History Skills

History Skills prepares students for the study of history in higher education and enables them to get the most out of their course. It advises on the nature of the discipline, and on what to look for when assessing the courses available. The bulk of the book is designed to help develop the key skills successful students will be expected to master. These are also skills which history graduates will deploy in their applications for a wide range of opportunities in employment and training.

History Skills represents the combined experience of tutors who have taught across the range of higher education institutions. It offers an unrivalled 'insider's view' of what it takes to succeed. Clear and practical advice helps students become more comfortable with the core elements of historical study, establishing the confidence needed to enjoy any course to the utmost.

Edited by Mary Abbott

History Skills
A student's handbook

London and New York

First published 1996
by Routledge
11 New Fetter Lane, London EC4P 4EE

Simultaneously published in the USA and Canada
by Routledge
29 West 35th Street, New York, NY 10001

Typeset in Times by Florencetype Limited, Stoodleigh, Devon

Printed and bound in Great Britain by Clays Ltd, St Ives PLC

British Library Cataloguing in Publication Data
A catalogue record for this book is available from the British Library.

Library of Congress Cataloguing in Publication Data
History skills / edited by Mary Abbott.
    Includes bibliographical references and index.
    1. History—Study and teaching (Secondary)—United States.
I. Abbott, Mary, 1942–
                D16.3.H54 1996   96-8249
                907.1'273—dc20   CIP

ISBN 0-415-11630-9

Contents

1
The historian's territory
Mary Abbott

This chapter explores the evolution of academic history. It is designed to help you get a head start in answering the question: 'What is history?' which many of you will face – in one form or another – as first-year undergraduates.

A passion for the past

Evidence of a widespread interest in and engagement with the past abounds in many shapes and forms.

Open the 'lifestyle' section of your paper on a Sunday morning and you'll come across articles with headings like 'Where to buy the Regency look' or 'Cook a meal to please Mr Darcy's palate'. Reviews in the arts pages may contain barbed (or, less often, positive) comment on the 'heritage' sideshows and merchandise which are so often by-products of art exhibitions. To take one example from 1996, those visitors to Lord Leighton's London studio who chose to assume the role of late nineteenth-century connoisseurs might (for an extra charge) sip champagne as they contemplated the female nude on canvas and in the flesh (a live model was engaged to add a further note of 'authenticity' to the re-creation of a fashionable Victorian painter's working environment).

Scan the shelves of W. H. Smith's and you will encounter magazines with titles like *Best of British*; *Family History Monthly*; *Heritage: A Celebration of Britain*; *History Today*; *Scottish Memorials* and *Yesterday: Stories and Pictures from the Past*.

National Trust and Past Times shops and catalogues purvey facsimiles and pastiches of books, artefacts and sounds.

On Bank Holidays re-enactments of Civil War battles and skirmishes, sometimes on or near the original site, the simulation of a day in the life a Tudor household, rallies of veteran cars and flying displays of historic aircraft are among the events that draw big crowds. If you choose instead to visit Cadbury's World at Bourneville just outside Birmingham, you'll travel through time from sixteenth-century Mexico to twentieth-century England. As you arrive, you'll be greeted with a version of the spicy chocolate drink which the Spanish *conquistadors* introduced to Europe. Later on, you'll watch hard- and soft-centres being 'enrobed' in chocolate and decorated on a production line of a kind long displaced from the main factory by more sophisticated technology.

County Record Offices are crowded with spare-time investigators dedicated to tracing their ancestry or collecting evidence relating to their home town or village. Other enthusiasts devote their leisure to the painstaking restoration of examples of machinery overtaken by revolutions in technology. Windmills are an obvious example.

A passionate involvement with the past may have far-reaching consequences for the world we live in today. The end walls of terraced houses in 'loyalist' areas of Belfast, decorated with polychrome images of 'King Billy' who slew the papish crew at the Battle of Boyne Water in 1691, are icons of their makers' political allegiance.

How do these very diverse manifestations of our apparently insatiable appetite for the past relate to the territory occupied by professional historians? This is a difficult question to which I shall return later in the chapter. For the moment, it is worth bearing in mind that the broad umbrella of history shelters – often mutually suspicious – practitioners committed to an extraordinary range of projects. The popular preoccupation with the past has itself become the subject of the historian's scrutiny: in 1994 Raphael Samuel published a large and deliberately repetitious collection of essays under the title *Theatres of Memory: Past and Present in Contemporary Culture*.

The history of history

This section reviews some key dimensions of the developing tradition of writing about the past (sometimes the very recent past) in England from the Middle Ages to the present day. Advocates of equal opportunities will be struck by the under-representation of women. This is a fact of history which feminists (male and female) must come to terms with: it is not open-and-shut evidence of a conscious male conspiracy.

The survey which follows does not pretend to be a comprehensive overview of the historian's approaches or sources (turn to Chapter 3, 'Sources and resources', for a fuller discussion of the historian's raw materials). **It is intended to help you to develop an understanding of the criteria which define academic history and, at times, separate it from the popular passion for the past.**

Rather than paraphrase the perspectives from which writers have approached the past, I have given their views in their own words. If you've seen *The Usual Suspects***, you'll be alert to the risks of accepting uncorroborated testimony. Historians learned this lesson long ago. It is this wariness which accounts for our emphasis on** *referencing* **in Chapters 4 and 5, 'Note making and Essay writing', and on the full panoply of** *scholarly apparatus* **in Chapter 8, 'Research methods'.**

If you're not used to reading seventeenth-, eighteenth- or nineteenth-century prose and find the (indented) passages of quotation hard to handle because of the language they are written in, you can skip over them to my comments and track back to see whether I have provided you with convincing evidence of the points I've made. To get a quick, rather telegraphic, overview, you could scan the chapter for the sentences and phrases printed in bold type. (If you haven't already done so, it's worth developing a range of reading strategies – we return to this topic in Chapter 4.) Where words or phrases are in bold type, the emphasis is mine, not the original author's.

I have chosen to illustrate and discuss these key dimensions under the following headings:

- the Christian tradition
- the antiquarian tradition
- the heritage of the ancient world
- the Whig tradition
- the 'scientific revolution' of the nineteenth century
- social science
- the Marxist tradition
- history today

It would be a mistake to think of these ways of writing about the past as the historical equivalent of geological strata. They are not discrete. They coexist in time and in the terms of reference which writers employ in their work. I have choosen Thomas Babington Macaulay (1800–1859) to exemplify the Whig tradition. As a Whig, he wrote within a Christian – specifically a Protestant – framework. And as author of the *Lays of Ancient Rome*, he helped to shape the popular idea of the ancient world. Macaulay was a frequent contributor to journals intended for the serious general reader; he served, in India, as an officer of the East India Company and, in Britain, as an MP and cabinet minister before retiring in his early forties to devote his life to writing. Until the later nineteenth century, when the historian's craft was professionalised, writing about the past was the province of the churchman, the gentleman (much less frequently the gentlewoman) of independent means and the hack. From the sixteenth century on, many of these men were university-educated (Macaulay was a Cambridge man), but few were university-based.

The Christian tradition

Outline histories of the history which has been written in the West generally begin with the ancient Greeks. I propose to start instead with an English writer, Bede, who was born in Northumbria in or about the year 673 and wrote (in Latin) *A History of the English Church and People*. In his Preface Bede outlines the authorities on which his text is based (I am quoting from the translation originally published by Penguin in 1955):

> in order to avoid any doubts in the mind of yourself, or any who may listen to or read this history, as to the accuracy of what I have written, allow me briefly to state the authorities upon whom I chiefly depend.
>
> My principal authority and adviser in this work has been the most reverend Abbot Albinus, an eminent scholar educated in the church of Canterbury by Archbishop Theodore and Abbot Hadrian, both of them respected and learned men. He carefully transmitted to me verbally or in writing through Nothelm, a priest of the church of London, anything he considered worthy of mention that had been done by disciples of the blessed Pope Gregory in the province of Kent or in the surrounding regions. Such facts he ascertained either from records or from the recollections of older men. Nothelm himself later visited Rome, and obtained permission from the present Pope Gregory (II) to examine the archives of the holy Roman Church. He found there

letters of Pope Gregory (I) and other Popes, and when he returned, the reverend Father Albinus advised him to bring them to me for inclusion in this history. So for the period at which this volume begins until the time when the English nation received the Faith of Christ, I have drawn extensively on the works of earlier writers gathered from various sources.

The materials on which Bede drew were not uniform. Thus on his home ground:

> With regard to events in the various districts of the province of the Northumbrians, from the time that it received the Faith of Christ up to the present day, I am not dependent on any one author, but on countless faithful witnesses who either know or remember the facts, apart from what I know myself.

It is the attention Bede pays to ensuring 'the accuracy' of his account and citing 'the authorities ... upon whom [he] chiefly depend[ed]' that have led historians of history – more formally known as historiographers – to accept the title of his *History* as a label appropriate to its contents.

The emphasis on the authority of churchmen and the references to the progressive conversion of the English people to 'the Faith of Christ' are important clues to Bede's **interpretation of the evidence** before him. The Preface, written by 'Bede the Priest and Servant of Christ' and addressed 'To the Most Glorious King Ceolwulf' – of Northumbria – spells out his agenda.

> I warmly welcome the diligent zeal and sincerity with which you study the words of Holy Scripture and your eager desire to know something of the doings and sayings of men of the past, and of famous men of our own nation in particular. For if history records good things of good men, the thoughtful hearer is encouraged to imitate what is good; or if it records evil of wicked men, the devout, religious listener or reader is encouraged to avoid all that is sinful and perverse and to follow what he knows to be good and pleasing to God.

Most historians, whether they acknowledge it or not, are partisan. Here goodness is equated with 'the Faith of Christ', perversity with the heathen. The text I have quoted makes crystal clear **the perspective from which he wrote**: Bede was a devout Christian, indeed a man brought up in a monastic community from early childhood. Bede's standpoint may provoke hostility or suspicion in the secular-minded but I would argue that **in making his allegiance explicit, Bede may be adopting a more intellectually honest position than later academics who have pretended to a quasi-scientific objectivity.**

In Bede's day – and for the better part of the next millennium – the Bible was accepted as a literally true record of past events and an accurate, if obscure, predictor of what was to come. The Act of Creation and the Day of Judgement were recognised as the temporal boundaries of human existence. The most eminent seventeenth-century scholars devoted their time to calculating the dates of the beginning and end of the world: on the basis of scriptural evidence, Henry Ussher (died 1613) dated Creation to the year 4004 BC.

From the time of the conversion of the English rulers, which Bede describes, until the twentieth century, most writing about the past was the work of men who subscribed to the tenets of the state-supported Church which, before and after the separation of the Church in England from the Church of Rome in the 1530s, endorsed the superiority of Christian over heathen, Muslim or Jew, lord over labourer, man over woman. Biblical allusions, which those of us brought up in the secular second half of the twentieth century have to look up, were second nature to the authors, readers and hearers of accounts of the past written a hundred, five hundred, a thousand years ago. As Paul Fussell demonstrates in *The Great War and Modern Memory* (Oxford, 1975), the image of Christ crucified, the pattern of unmerited suffering, was a natural metaphor for Wilfred Owen, Siegfried Sassoon and the less well-known makers of 'countless Great War poems'.

The persistent use of BC (Before Christ) and AD (Anno Domini – in the Year of Our Lord) to define **time, that essential axis of historical investigation**, is a daily reminder of the significance of Christianity for our understanding of the history of Western Europe.

Bede's **interpretation of** the **events** he describes is **informed by the assumptions of his own day**. He believed in miracles.

Here is the core of his account of an episode in the life of Germanus, bishop of Auxerre (died 448), who twice visited Britain – in 429 and 440 – to campaign against heretics. While Germanus 'was disabled and helpless', laid up with a broken leg,

> fire broke out in a cottage near his lodging, and ... was carried by the wind to the cottage where he lay. The people ran to pick up the bishop and carry him to a place of safety; but, full of trust in God,

he reproved them and would not allow them to do so ... the flames
... raged all around it, [but] the place that sheltered him stood
untouched amid a sea of fire.

**Responding to the challenge of different world views is among the most
demanding and exciting intellectual and imaginative aspects of the
historian's craft.**

The antiquarian tradition

The earliest English antiquaries were influenced by the fifteenth-century Italian scholars who devoted their lives to the study of antiquity:
the literary and archaeological remains of ancient Rome.

John Leland (died 1552) was England's most distinguished pioneer
of this tradition. Henry VIII appointed him King's Antiquary, 'in which
office', to quote the *Dictionary of National Biography* (usually referred
to as *DNB*, a monument to Victorian scholarship and still **an invaluable tool for the historian**), 'he had neither predecessor or successor'.

Leland was educated at St Paul's School in London, academically the
most progressive school of its day (in England); at Christ's College,
Cambridge; at All Souls, Oxford, and in Paris. 'He returned' – says the
DNB – 'a finished scholar in both Latin and Greek'. Back in England
he undertook a great itinerary, or tour, in search of ancient monuments
but the project to which he devoted his life – the history and antiquities of his homeland – was never completed and very little of his work
went into print. Leland's manuscripts did, however, influence the growing number of men, often but not invariably university-educated, who
pursued the past in the antiquarian mode, **recording, preserving, order-
ing and indexing the material they gathered, rather than *interpreting* it.**

I have chosen as my exemplary antiquarian the prodigiously indus-
trious William Dugdale (1605–1686). Dugdale did not go to university.
He married at 18, to please his elderly father who was anxious to see
his son and property settled.

Like Leland, Dugdale was interested in artefacts, and, as a herald and
official rooter-out of those who laid false claim to coats of arms, in armo-
rial and genealogical evidence in particular. My quotations come from
*The Life of that Learned Antiquary Sir William Dugdale, Knight, Garter
Principal, King of Arms*, published in 1713.

The Printed Books by him [that is 'written by him'] given to the
Heralds' Office are these, viz [videlicet – 'that is to say'. Viz. is a now

rarely used cousin of i.e., which also means 'that is' and, is like viz., derived from Latin – i[d] e[st]]

1 *The Antiquities of Warwickshire* Illustrated
2 The *Monasticon Anglicanum* in Three Volumes
3 *The History of St Paul's Cathedral*
4 *The History of Imbanking and Draining the Fenns*
5 His Book Intituled *Origines Juridiciales*
6 His Two Volumes of the *Baronage* of England.

His Collections of Materials from the Records in the Tower of London, the Rolls of Chancery Lane, the Treasury of the Exchequer, the King's Remembrancer's Office and other Places; as also for Leiger Books and Ancient Manuscripts in the Famous Cottonian [a private collection which became a part of the British Library] and Bodleian [the Library of Oxford University] Libraries; likewise from a Multitude of Original Charters of which he did make use in Compiling his Historical Work of Warwickshire Antiquities and the Baronage of England, all gathered and written with his own hand, and are in Number no less than Twenty-seven Volumes in Folio; all of which, to be preserved for Posterity, he hath given by his last Will and Testament to the University of Oxford.

The antiquarian approach to the study of the past remained significant and highly regarded well into the nineteenth century. Evelyn Shirley (1812–1882), a kinsman of Dugdale's associate Thomas Shirley, was educated at Oxford but it was his estate at Ettington, a property held by his forebears in unbroken male line since the time of the Domesday Inquest in 1086, which inspired him to amass and publish a huge collection of evidence for the history of his family under the title *Stemmata Shirleiana* ('The Shirley line') in 1841. A second revised and enlarged edition of *Stemmata Shirleiana* came out in 1873.

Dugdale's *Monasticon*, revised and enlarged in 1817 with 'the General Reader, the Antiquary and the Lawyer' as its target market, was reprinted in 1970 and remains an important resource for students of medieval England.

Today 'antiquarian' and 'antiquarianism' are often used pejoratively – that's to say in a deprecating way – but I would argue that historians have cause to be grateful to the painstaking copyists whose contribution to the academic study of the past has been to preserve evidence and make it available to others. The many, many lay men and women who cooperated with professional demographers in the great project of recovering the English evidence for population figures and trends between the sixteenth and the early nineteenth century provide a recent example. Without their transcriptions of the records of baptisms, burials and marriages from parish registers, the sophisticated analysis and interpretation of these data would not have occurred. Their monument is *The Population History of England and Wales, 1541–1871: A Reconstruction* by E. A. Wrigley and R. S. Schofield; the most recent edition was published by Cambridge University Press in 1989. **The application of statistics to history is the subject of Chapter 9.**

The heritage of the ancient world

There are strong indications (but no convincing statistical proof) that the later sixteenth century saw a surge of Latin literacy, particularly among the ranks of landowners, bureaucrats and professional men. (A minority of these privileged men were able to read Greek too.) This rise in literacy was linked to a rediscovery of ancient literature, the proliferation of printed texts and a new emphasis on formal academic education at grammar schools and the universities (of Oxford and Cambridge) for the sons of landowners and the better-off professional and businessmen. Those whose reading was confined to the vernacular (mother tongue) had access to the works of ancient authors in translation and in simplified versions. The frontispiece to the edition of *Dr Goldsmith's Roman History abridged by himself for the Use of Schools*, published in 1801, is decorated with a rather crude woodcut of a wolf suckling two small children. Predictably, Chapter 1 includes the account of the infancy of Romulus and Remus. Twin sons of the god Mars and Rhea Sylvia, a vestal virgin 'condemned to be buried alive, the usual punishment for Vestals who had violated their chastity', the babies were cast out to die.

A wolf descending from the mountain to drink, ran, at the cry of the children, and gave them suck under a fig-tree; caressing and licking them as if they had been her own young; the infants hanging on her dugs as if she had been their mother; until Faustulus, the king's shepherd, struck with so surprising a sight, conveyed them home, and delivered them to his wife Lucretia to nurse; who brought them up as her own. Some, however, will have it, that from the vicious life of this woman, the shepherds had given her the nick-name of *Lupa*, or wolf, which they suppose might possibly be the occasion of this marvellous story.

Many of Goldsmith's middle- and upper-class readers would have been familiar with stories from Greece and Rome from their nursery days: the letter X, a perennial challenge to the makers of alphabet games, was frequently represented in the eighteenth century by Socrates' wife Xanthippe, the stereotypical scold.

This perspective on the past is much more than a mere category of historical production and consumption; the Graeco-Roman heritage suffused the lives of many English men and boys from the sixteenth to the twentieth century.

As Christian writers celebrated the conversion of the heathen, the Greeks and the Romans celebrated patriotism and the triumph of civilisation over barbarism. The work of ancient writers was used to train the youth of England, not merely in civic virtues but in military tactics and strategy. *The Complete Captain or an Abbridgement of Cesar's Warres with Observations upon them*, in fact the Englished version of a French text, is an example of the genre. It was conceived, as its title suggests, as a manual for the professional soldier. (The edition I am using was published with the imprimatur [permission to print] of the University of Cambridge in 1640.) In commenting on Caesar's second expedition to Britain in 54 BC, the Duc de Rohan (1579–1638), a French commander whose forces trounced the Spanish army in 1635, observed:

> In this second voyage of Cesar into Britain, though he went thither with greater forces and better prepared then [than] at first, having supplied those defects which were wanting before; nevertheless going into a countrey which he could not come to but by sea, where he had no intelligence [in the Secret Service sense], and going from another newly conquered, subject to revoltings, and which grudgingly endured subjection, he rather therein satisfied his own ambition, than that he added any great profit to the Romanes.

Edward Gibbon's *Decline and Fall of the Roman Empire*, published between 1776 and 1788, is the most celebrated and sophisticated expression of the classical tradition of writing about the past.

Gibbon (1737–1794) was not a university academic. Indeed, as he confided in his *Memoirs*,

> To the University of Oxford I acknowledge no obligation; and she will cheerfully renounce me for a son, as I am willing to disclaim

her for mother. I spent fourteen months at Magdalen College; they proved the fourteen months the most idle and unprofitable of my whole life.

Nor was he a miner of archives: a gentleman of leisure, he pursued his researches among the printed texts in his own 'house and library'.

The *Decline and Fall* was an immediate popular and critical triumph. In Gibbon's own words:

I am at a loss to describe the success of the work, without betraying the vanity of the writer. The first impression was exhausted in a few days; a second and third edition were scarcely adequate to the demand; and the bookseller's property was twice invaded by the pirates of Dublin. My book was on every table, and almost on every toilette [lady's dressing table]; the historian was crowned by the taste or fashion of the day; nor was the general voice disturbed by the barking of any profane critic.

To my mind, in Gibbon are combined **the literary skills of a master of English prose and the forensic skills of a coroner presiding over a post-mortem** – two splendid qualities in a historian's armoury. Taste Gibbon's text and judge him for yourself. This is his opening paragraph:

In the second century of the Christian era, the empire of Rome com-prehended the fairest part of the earth, and the most civilised por-tion of mankind. The frontiers of that extensive monarchy were guarded by ancient renown and disciplined valour. The gentle but powerful influence of laws and manners had gradually cemented the union of the provinces. Their peaceful inhabitants enjoyed and abused the advantages of wealth and luxury. The image of a free constitu-tion was preserved with decent reverence: the Roman Senate appeared to possess the sovereign authority, and devolved on the emperors all the executive powers of government. During a happy period (AD 98–180) of more than fourscore years, the public admin-istration was conducted by the virtue and ability of Nerva, Trajan, Hadrian, and the two Antonines. It is the design of this, and of the two succeeding chapters, to describe the prosperous condition of their empire; and afterwards, from the death of Marcus Antoninus, to deduce the most important circumstances of its decline and fall; a revolution which will ever be remembered, and is still felt by the nations of the earth.

The attentive reader immediately picks up the message that something is rotten in the state of Rome:

> Their peaceful inhabitants enjoyed and **abused** the advantages of wealth and **luxury**. The **image** of a free constitution was preserved with decent reverence: the Roman senate **appeared** to possess the sovereign authority, and devolved on the emperors all the executive powers of government.

The import of the decline and fall, **'a revolution which will ever be remembered, and is still felt by the nations of the earth'**, is clearly signalled.

Or take his character sketch of Julian the Apostate, which I have extracted from the first paragraph of Chapter XXIII (our use of Roman numerals is – of course – another small but enduring legacy from the ancient world):

> Our partial ignorance may represent him as a philosophic monarch, who studied to protect, with an equal hand, the religious factions of the empire, and to allay the theological fever which had inflamed the minds of the people. ... A more accurate view of the character and conduct of Julian will remove this favourable prepossession for a prince who did not escape the general contagion of the times. **We enjoy the singular advantage of comparing the pictures which have been delineated by his fondest admirers and his implacable enemies.**

This sense of identity with the ancients persisted until at least the 1920s. The memorable phrases and rhythms of Macaulay's *Lays of Ancient Rome* (1842) fixed some heroes' stories in the schoolboy's mind. Although, as he observed in his commentary,

> there can be little doubt that among those parts of early Roman history which had a poetical origin was the legend of Horatius Cocles. We have several versions of the story and these versions differ from each other in points of no small importance.

Macaulay's version of how Horatius, single-handed, held the bridge against the Etruscans is stirring indeed:

> All Rome sent forth a rapturous cry
> And even the ranks of Tuscany
> Could scarce forbear to cheer.

Just as the image of Christ crucified epitomised innocent suffering for the poets of the Great War, so classical parallels and sentiments sprang to their minds when they described gallantry and patriotism. Patrick Shaw-Stewart, who was killed in action in 1917, drew on Greek myths and legends for his untitled poem on Gallipoli, which ends with the lines

> Stand in the trench, Achilles,
> Flame-capped, and shout for me.

Wilfred Owen (1893–1918) used as the title and final words of what he called a 'gas poem', the famous Latin tag *Dulce et decorum est pro patria mori*. 'The old Lie', which, as he explained, in a letter to his mother Susan, 'means of course *It is sweet and meet to die for one's country. Sweet! and decorous!*'. *Dulce et decorum est pro patria mori* is inscribed, without Owen's bitter, ironic intention, on the War memorial which the Royal Grammar School at Newcastle upon Tyne erected to Owen's contemporaries, the Old Boys who died for their King and Country.

The Whig tradition

Writers in the Whig tradition saw England as 'top nation' and 'getting better all the time'. Thomas Babington Macaulay is my exemplar of a writer of Whig history. Macaulay's great Whig opus was *The History of England from the Accession of James II*, published in 1849. Macaulay's hero was James's nephew and son-in-law William III, who supplanted him in **1688**, an event Macaulay regarded as a **Glorious Revolution.**

England's perceived superiority had deep roots. From the standpoint of the beginning of Victoria's reign, Macaulay looked back to the thirteenth century when **Magna Carta** was forced out of King John and 'framed for their mutual benefit' by the 'united exertions' of the great grandsons of the men who confronted each other in the Battle of Hastings in 1066:

> It can easily be proved that, in our own land, **the national wealth has, during at least six centuries, been almost uninterruptedly increased**. ... **This progress became at length, about the middle of the eighteenth century, portentously rapid, and has proceeded during the nineteenth century with accelerated velocity.** In consequence, partly of our geographical and partly of our moral position, we have, during several generations been exempt from evils which have elsewhere impeded the efforts and destroyed the fruits of industry. ...

**Under the benignant influence of peace and liberty, science has flour-
ished, and has been applied to practical purposes on a scale never
before known.**

For Macaulay, the 1680s were the make-or-break decade on England's
path to greatness. Charles II, a monarch festooned with mistresses and
bastard sons, had no legitimate child. On his death, the crown passed
by default to his brother James, a more honest and less subtle man,
who, in contrast to the cleverer and more devious Charles, openly proclaimed his allegiance to the Church of Rome. His actions justified the
Dutch leader, William of Orange, already a hero in the eyes of
Protestant Europe, in staking his claim to the throne of England, as co-
sovereign with his wife Mary, King James's elder daughter. The
Convention Parliament met early in 1689, at William's invitation: it was
on the strength of a joint resolution of the Lords and Commons that
the throne was declared vacant and William and Mary were proclaimed
King and Queen.

The city of London led the way, and **elected**, without any contest,
four great merchants who were **zealous Whigs**. The king [James II]
and his adherents had hoped that many returning officers would treat
the prince's [William of Orange's] letter as a nullity; but the hope was
disappointed. The elections [to the Convention] went on rapidly and
smoothly. There was scarcely any contest. ... There was scarcely a
county in which the gentry and the yeomanry had not, many months
before, fixed upon candidates, **good Protestants** ... and these candidates were now generally returned without opposition.

The second volume of Macaulay's *History* ends with this resounding
assertion:

**For the authority of law, for the security of property, for the peace
of our streets, for the happiness of our homes, our gratitude is due,
under Him who raises and pulls down nations at his pleasure to the
Long Parliament [which confronted Charles I], to the Convention
and to William of Orange.**

The scientific revolution of the nineteenth century

Taken as a whole, historians' work has a short shelf-life. The man I have
chosen as the advocate of historical science is generally remembered
only for the aphorism 'Power tends to corrupt and absolute power

corrupts absolutely'. This tag, consciously or unconsciously, he picked up from Pitt the Elder, who, addressing the Lords in January 1770, declared that 'Unlimited power is apt to corrupt the minds of those who possess it'. Although it would please the subversive in us to catch an eminent Victorian out in the crime of **plagiarism (the unacknowledged use of another person's words or ideas)**, it is more likely that, in a private letter to the Professor of Ecclesiastical History in the University of Cambridge, Acton was sharing an allusion rather than stealing a concept.

John Emerich Edward Dahlberg Acton (1834–1902) was not a meritocrat, an example of Victorian self-help. He was the son of a German aristocrat and an English baronet; his step-father was an earl. Acton was not the product of an English university education, he was privately tutored in Munich – indeed, he thought of himself as 'never more than half an Englishman'. His experience of continental, specifically German, historians, put him in the position of mediator between the scientific school of German historians, led by Leopold von Ranke, and the English universities. For most of his life an independent scholar, he received honorary doctorates from the Universities of Munich, Oxford and Cambridge. 'On a hint from Gladstone', he was elected a Fellow of All Souls and, in 1895, appointed Regius Professor of Modern History at Cambridge.

In a tribute to his intellectual hero, Ranke, which appeared in the first article in the inaugural issue of *The English Historical Review* in 1886, Lord Acton epitomised the new 'scientific' attitude to history.

Ranke has not only written a larger number of mostly excellent books than any man that ever lived, but he has taken pains from the first to explain how the thing is done. He attained a position unparalleled in literature, less by the display of extraordinary faculties than by **perfect mastery** of the secret **of his craft**, and that secret he always made it his business to impart. For his most eminent predecessors, history was applied politics, fluid law, religion exemplified, or the school of patriotism. Ranke was the first German to pursue it for no purpose but its own. He tried to make the generality of educated men understand how it came about that the world of the fifteenth century was changed into the Europe of the nineteenth. His own definite persuasions regarding church and king were not suffered to permeate his books. . . .

He expects no professional knowledge in his readers, and never writes for specialists. . . . **As he writes history, not biography, he**

abstains from the secrets of private life; and as he writes history, not dogma, he never sorts men into black and white according to their bearing in vital controversies. His evil-doers escape the just rigour of the law, and he avoids hero-worship as the last ditch of prehistoric prejudice.

Social science

The twentieth-century historians who embraced this notion of objectivity were and continue to be open to the influence of the methodologies developed by practitioners of other 'social sciences'.

Today *Continuity and Change*, a history journal published by Cambridge University Press, advertises itself as a periodical which specialises in

> studies whose agenda or methodology combines elements from **traditional fields** such as history, **sociology, law, demography, economics or anthropology**, or ranges freely between them.

Among the most enduring memorials to the impact of social science on early twentieth-century historians is Alice Clark's *Working Life of Women in the Seventeenth Century* which came out in 1919. Alice Clark (born 1874) was a member of the Quaker family of shoe manufacturers and, until her health broke down when she was in her thirties, she was an active member of the family firm. At 38 she was awarded one of the bursaries endowed by Mrs Bernard Shaw at the London School of Economics and turned her 'attention to the circumstances of women's lives' in a period which she associated with 'the triumph of capitalistic organisation'.

Although she wrote within a Christian humanitarian framework, Clark's belief in 'the triumph of capitalistic organisation' links her work to the Marxist tradition. From the point of view of theory, Marx has been the most potent influence on the making of English histories in the twentieth century.

The Marxist tradition

Marxist historians see the past in terms of **class struggle**. For Marx, class was determined not by the conventional markers of wealth, power and status but was **the outcome of economic roles, 'the relations of production'**.

The classic statement of Marx's definition of the basis of class formation comes from the Preface of *A Contribution to the Critique of Political Economy*:

> The totality of these relations of production constitutes the economic structure of society, the real foundation, on which arises a legal and political superstructure and to which correspond definite forms of social consciousness. The mode of production of material life conditions the general process of social, political and intellectual life. It is not the consciousness of men that determines their existence, but their social existence that determines their consciousness.

To the Marxist tradition belong two of the most charismatic English historians of the twentieth century: Christopher Hill (born 1912), who argued that the English Civil War was 'a class war' between the Crown, backed by conservative landlords and the established Church, and 'the trading and industrial classes in town and countryside'; and Edward Palmer Thompson. It is perhaps worth noting in passing that their wives, Bridget Hill and Dorothy Thompson, are distinguished historians in their own right. In the last 25 years women have become much more significant in the practice of history – both as researchers and as the subjects of research.

E. P. Thompson (1924–1993), whom I have chosen as my exemplar of the British Marxist tradition, joined the Communist Party while he was an undergraduate at Cambridge. War service interrupted his studies. After the war, as he describes in his book *The Railway – an Adventure in Construction* (1948), he did voluntary work in Bulgaria and Yugoslavia. His first major academic work was on William Morris (1834–1896), the English socialist and visionary. Unlike Hill, who spent his whole academic career at Oxford, Thompson taught in adult education in the north of England until, in 1965, he became Reader in Social History at the University of Warwick. He gave up university work after ten years or so to write and to work for the Campaign for Nuclear Disarmament.

The book on which E. P. Thompson's reputation rests, The *Making of the English Working Class*, was first published in 1963. The passages I reproduce are quoted from the Pelican edition of 1968. Thompson lays out his thesis in his Preface:

In the years between 1780 and 1832 most English working people came to feel an identity of interest between themselves, and against

their rulers and employers. This **ruling class** was itself much divided, and in fact only gained in cohesion over the same years because certain **antagonisms were resolved (or faded into insignificance) in the face of an insurgent working class**. Thus the working-class presence was, in 1832 [the year of the Great Reform Act], the most significant factor in British political life.

Thompson saw it as his mission to

rescue the poor stockinger, the Luddite cropper, the 'obsolete' hand-loom weaver, the 'utopian' artisan and even the deluded follower of Joanna Southcott*, from the enormous condescension of posterity. Their crafts and traditions may have been dying. Their hostility to the new industrialism may have been backward-looking. Their communitarian ideals may have been fantasies. Their insurrectionary conspiracies may have been foolhardy. But they lived through these times of acute social disturbance, and we did not. **Their aspirations were valid in terms of their own experience**.

* Joanna Southcott (1750–1814) was a prophetess who produced a string of religious pamphlets stressing the role of women in the Bible. She died believing she was pregnant with Jesus Christ.

History today

As Thompson's list suggests, the Marxist approach is intimately linked to a commitment to write **history from below – the history of the traditionally under-privileged and under-represented – the poor, the female and, increasingly, the black members of society.**

In the words of Raphael Samuel, one of its founding fathers, History Workshop, an important vehicle for the extension of the historian's portfolio, began life at a time 'when **the cultural revolution of the 1960s** was seemingly carrying all before it'. Its cradle was Ruskin College, Oxford, 'a trade union college, largely recruited from young workers; ... very responsive to the student revolt of 1968, and in fact, ... out on strike some days before the May Events in Paris. ... Another slightly later influence on the Workshop was the **women's movement**.'

From the outset, Samuel explained, the Workshop philosophy was that

anything could be studied provided one was adventurous enough in discovering original documents or new sources, and diligent in following up leads. (One of the appeals of **oral history** [based on spoken, as opposed to written, testimony], introduced to the Workshop in 1969, was that it enormously enlarged the field.)

The *History Workshop Journal*, launched in 1976, described itself as a 'journal of socialist historians'. In keeping with the Workshop philosophy, it pursued a wide agenda but, as Samuel observed in 1991, looking back at its first fifteen years of publication, it 'sets great store by **footnotes**' and the **'punctilio' of scholarly apparatus** – 'it is inescapably a learned journal'.

Issue One of *History Workshop Journal* included an article on 'Feminist history' by Sally Alexander and Anna Davin.

> We are arguing for **a political perspective in historical research and writing**, a suggestion which must disturb every academic vigilant in pursuit of the 'value-free'. But we announce our perspective and our values, thus showing greater respect for the critical faculties of our readers, and perhaps greater self-awareness than the unguarded vigilant.

In 1981 the *History Workshop Journal* began to describe itself as 'a journal of socialist and feminist historians'.

Currently, historians' concern with gender bias in the study of the past is expressed not simply in terms of masculinity/femininity but in terms of heterosexuality/homosexuality – particularly by lesbian and gay writers.

In March 1996 Catherine Hall, Professor of Sociology at the University of Essex, published a piece in the *Times Higher Education Supplement* – the academic's trade paper – under the title 'The ruinous ghost of empire past'. She took Cadbury's World as a peg on which to hang her discussion of the neglect of race in history. Here is her final paragraph:

> Cadbury's, its products, its story, is part of the world of our **raced imaginations, part of our tastes, part of our collective memories, part of our classed and gendered identities, part of how histories work in the present**. At Cadbury's World this raced history is uneasily occluded. A benign version of the past reigns, located around notions of modernity and progress, forgetting expropriation and exploitation. If members of Britain's multi-ethnic population are to be full participants in the society of the millennium then blind eyes must be opened – for opening eyes wider might enable us to see and understand differently.

Notice how history keeps escaping from the confines of the library and the classroom into the real world.

Ruth Richardson's work is another instance of the way in which the boundaries of historical investigation have been pushed back. *Death, Dissection and the Destitute* was published in 1988. As she wrote in her Introduction:

> I believe that my findings are important, and for this reason: the story of the Anatomy Act [of 1832] has never properly been told. Death studies as a discipline are in their infancy in Britain, and other social historians of death since 1800 have so far overlooked the Act entirely. References by social and economic historians to the Act's existence are scanty. Historians of government growth and administrative history hardly mention it, I have found only one who has noticed that the 1832 Anatomy Act established the earliest centrally funded and administered Inspectorate of . . . nineteenth-century administrative reform. Poor Law historians often assume that popular beliefs associated with the mutilation [or] maltreatment of the workhouse dead have no basis in rationality or fact. Historians of medicine greet the Act with little comprehension of its social meaning beyond the material interests of the medical profession. They omit to address the question of what the return effects might be upon the profession's body of anatomical knowledge that it is based upon bodies obtained by coercion.

In keeping with her claim that her **'findings are important'**, this short paragraph is **supported by** no fewer than seven **footnotes**.

She concludes her study with this statement:

> the fact of dissection which stands behind [the] fearsome reputation [of the pauper funeral] has been cloaked in silence. Over the course of Victoria's reign, the fact that the misfortune of poverty could qualify a person for dismemberment after death became too intensely painful for contemplation; became taboo. The memory went underground of a fate literally unspeakable . . .

Like a number of other significant historians of today – Simon Schama is perhaps the outstanding example – Ruth Richardson brings her own experience directly to bear on her research and writing. Among her Acknowledgements in *Death, Dissection and the Destitute* is one to

> the first teacher I met who didn't pretend to an omnipotence of knowledge. His admission of ignorance taught me at one stroke the

integrity of an honest humility and the possible value of my own knowledge and intuitions.

Acknowledgements to teachers, family and friends, colleagues and students are commonplace; it is to the content of the acknowledgement that I want to draw to your attention.

In the Introduction Richardson links her personal memories with her historical project:

> As a child in the mid-50s in London's Notting Hill, I can clearly remember the local belief that the chimney of a nearby hospital (an old workhouse infirmary) belched out the smoke of human fuel.

Death, Dissection and the Destitute is thus, in a sense, the academic explanation of a myth of the urban playground.

To return to the question I posed at the start of the chapter: how does the popular appetite for the past relate to the territory occupied by the professional historian? It is not subject matter or source or approach – given the variety of approaches mentioned in this chapter, we might take as our motto a quip made by Oscar Wilde (1854–1900): **The one duty we owe to history is to rewrite it** – but the commitment to interrogate the evidence and interpretations of our sources and to provide readers with the means of checking out our conclusions for themselves that gives us the right to claim the title 'historian'.

2
Choosing a course
Mary Abbott

The wealth of choices outlined in directories and reviews of degree courses in or including history – the UCAS handbook or, indeed, *History Today*'s annual survey 'British university history now', might easily leave you feeling bewildered and 'spoilt for choice'. This chapter is designed to help you draw up a shortlist. Many of the factors would apply whatever subject you plan to study. The chapter is divided into two sections, the first of which focuses on the importance of making a realistic assessment of **your priorities and circumstances**; the short second section addresses **sources of evidence about degrees in history**. If you'd prefer to read the second section first, do. Historians need to develop – but use with a certain discrimination – the skill of ruthless reading. The process of choosing a history course is likely to be much messier than the model described here but the proposition that you invest time and thought in choosing the course which 'fits' you best is undoubtedly sound.

Your priorities and circumstances

It makes sense to take a long hard look at yourself. You will need to put these factors into an order of priority:

- academic and other interests and preferences
- course structure
- entry requirements
- family responsibilities

- financial considerations
- profile of students
- prospects for employment
- the reputation of the university or the department

Academic and other interests and preferences

If you take chronological coverage, geographical range and intellectual approaches into consideration, you'll recognise that very few institutions offer a truly comprehensive history programme. Some distinguished institutions – the School of Oriental and African Studies, for instance – have very distinct and focused portfolios. Others barely venture beyond Europe and the United States. Many universities offer little or nothing in the way of ancient or medieval history. Ask yourself which universities and colleges offer programmes which reflect your current interests and provide the richest opportunities to develop and extend them.

At the moment you may see yourself as a Single Honours student, concentrating your attentions on history, as a Joint Honours student, taking history and sociology, for example, or a Combined Honours student taking history alongside a wider range of related subjects. Which universities can accommodate your preference? Is there scope to change the balance of your programme in line with your intellectual development? Which universities would give you a chance to taste new subjects? What about technical skills relevant to the practice of history? Statistics, information technology and foreign languages are obvious examples.

Alongside your current and potential academic interests, you'll want to think about life outside the lecture theatre and library. How would you choose to spend your spare time? What might universities offer in the way of clubs and societies? Would you prefer a 'greenfield' campus – like the University of East Anglia – or a metropolitan setting – like Manchester or Leeds – or a small historic town – like Exeter? If you are a keen mountaineer, East Anglia will have little to offer you; if sailing is your life blood, is Birmingham the place for you?

Do you want to go away from home to study? If so, how far from home would you like to be? For many students, the ideal seems to be: near enough to come home sometimes for Sunday lunch but far enough away to deter parents from dropping in to see you without prior warning.

Course structure

At least on paper, the shape of higher education courses has been transformed in recent years. Some institutions have moved away from term-based to semester-based calendars – just as 'term' signals three blocks of study in a year, 'semester' signals two.

Many undergraduate programmes are now modular: that is they are composed of discrete units of study, each of which is credit-rated so that, as they pass the modules, students build up credits towards the award of an Honours degree (usually 360 credits). In modular programmes there are likely to be two or three assessment points in the course of the year rather than end-of-year exams or the 'big bang' of final examinations. There is often more variety in the modes of assessment used on modular degrees.

If, for personal or financial reasons, a student has to withdraw from a modular programme before she graduates, she carries with her the credit she has accumulated. This accumulated academic credit may be sufficient to qualify for an intermediate award – a Certificate of Higher Education (120 credits) or a Diploma of Higher Education (240 credits), for example. In a general sense, academic credits are recognised by all British universities; in practice, however, their currency varies from institution to institution and from course to course.

In large modular programmes, students enjoy a very wide range of choice. A student who specialises in cultural history might want to include modules on art history, film, literature and philosophy in her agreed programme of studies. A student interested in gender might wish to scan the university's catalogue of modules for related topics offered by other disciplines. And, though demand from students registered for an award in art and design might make this more problematic, a keen and accomplished amateur photographer might be able to gain academic credit while acquiring technical skills relevant to her leisure interest.

Entry requirements – formal

You will need to assess how you measure up to the standard entry requirements of the courses which attract you. What standard offers do admissions tutors make? Are you going to make the grade? If you are at school or college, take your tutor's advice.

Can you benefit from institutional links? If you are 17 or 18, is there a compact (an agreement) between your school or college and a university which guarantees you special consideration, perhaps in return for attending briefing sessions on higher education and completing tasks which should help you prepare yourself for it? If you are an Access student, does your course have a special relationship with any providers of higher education?

If you are not currently in education, your public library should be able to provide information about any educational guidance services for adults in your area. Most universities and colleges of further education offer general and individual information and advice on preparing for higher education.

If you are a mature person with a developed interest and expertise in a particular field – the history of your own family or locality, for instance, you may not find the scope of an undergraduate programme attractive. Universities may be prepared to consider you for a taught Master's degree, especially if you can provide evidence, in the form of published articles or written versions of papers you have given, of your ability to analyse, interpret and contextualise your findings.

Entry requirements – informal

Even if you have, or expect to achieve, a formal qualification in history at A level or an equivalent standard, it is important to realise that this is not what we sometimes call a 'necessary or sufficient' criterion for admission to a degree course in history. In other words, if you haven't got a formal qualification in history, you won't automatically be rejected; and if you have, you won't automatically be offered a place on the strength of your A level or Access Certificate alone.

A formal qualification in a related area – English literature, history of art, sociology, women's studies – may well be acceptable as an alternative and is almost certain to be seen as something that strengthens your application. If you are not applying as a school or college leaver, you may be able to demonstrate experience acquired outside the classroom which will help to convince an admissions tutor that you have the basic competencies to cope with taking lecture notes, researching topics and writing essays. Writing effective minutes and reports, whether these are tasks you have undertaken at work or in a voluntary capacity, could provide evidence of relevant skills.

Admissions tutors will look for evidence of serious commitment to the study of history – so that technical skills and paper qualifications provide only part of the evidence on which they will form their judgement of your ability to survive and thrive as an undergraduate historian. The reference from your tutor (if you are, or recently have been, at school or college) or from someone who can make a reasonably informed estimate of your potential (if you are not) is an important ingredient. But it is your own contribution to the application form which is crucial. Whether you are 18 or 49 when you apply to read history as all or part of your degree course, you'll need to be able to demonstrate, in a few well-honed sentences, that you have a basic understanding of the historian's territory and the energy and enthusiasm to devote a substantial proportion of your time over the next three years to the study of history. One obvious test is whether you carry your interest in history outside the classroom.

Family responsibilities and financial considerations

Many students have family responsibilities, and this isn't a peculiarity of mature students. A 20-year-old may find himself or herself caring for a child or an elderly relative, or functioning as a key member of a family enterprise – a shop, a garage, a pub. A 50-year-old can be fancy-free.

If you have commitments at home, find out whether your local colleges and universities take family responsibilities into account in timetabling lectures and other classes. Is there a nursery? Does the university run an after-school club for older children? How will you cope at half term?

Students' maintenance grants have not kept pace with inflation. And they are means-tested – the incomes of parents and spouses are taken into account.

You may need to investigate the level of rents charged in university halls of residence and in the private sector. If shortage of money means that going away to university is out of the question, what are the opportunities close to home? The growth of franchise arrangements between universities and colleges of further and higher education means that it is often possible at least to begin your studies in a college close to your home. The choice of options is likely to be smaller than on the main campus of a university.

If you know in advance that you will need to supplement your grant, find out about the university's policy on part-time paid employment during academic sessions. Will the university help you to find paid work? (Opportunities for part-time bar and catering work in the evenings and at weekends are probably greatest in towns and cities which attract tourists all the year round.)

Profile of students

Some institutions have very diverse student populations: they recruit people in a wide age band and with a wide range of educational and cultural backgrounds. Others have student bodies of a more traditional kind and the school or college leaver with an A level in history predominates. Where would you feel happier?

Special needs

If you are likely to need extra support because you have learning difficulties, a medical condition, or physical or sensory impairment of any kind, get in touch with the university as long as possible before you are due to make a formal application. This will give you a chance to assess whether the university's equal opportunities policy is worth the paper it is written on and it will give the university and the course a chance to undertake any small works (such as a ramp to give easier access to a specialist room) or, for instance, to have material brailled or taped.

Prospects for employment

It is much harder to get a firm footing in the world of work than it used to be. What 'employment edge' will the university or course give you? Work placements and work-related skills – both technical things like information technology (IT) and foreign languages and the organisational ability acquired as a club treasurer or publicity officer – can make the difference between being selected for a shortlist or consigned to the notorious cylindrical filing basket under someone's desk.

The reputation of the university and/or the department

Reputation often lags behind reality. The academic historians who regularly appear on radio or television may have relatively little contact with the undergraduates in their home universities. They may be occupied with graduate students, their own research or their media careers. Occasional eminent historians make their lack of interest in teaching clear to their students by their perfunctory performance.

Because historians are naturally curious and sceptical people, you will naturally want to seek evidence for the reality that lies behind the reputation. The next section of the chapter outlines sources of information on all the issues I have outlined so far.

Sources of evidence

- UCAS Handbook
- Commercially published guides to higher education
- University prospectuses and course-specific literature
- Open days and interviews

UCAS Handbook   The UCAS Handbook is published by the clearing house which handles the great bulk of applications for undergraduate places in higher education. It is widely available in schools and colleges, through careers and guidance services and the reference departments of public libraries.

Commercially published guides to higher education   The same institutions generally also hold copies of commercially produced guides to higher education. *Which University?*, published by Push, provides not always flattering thumbnail sketches of institutions. *Which Degree?*, published by CRAC, has a section on history courses which includes course outlines. Brian Heap's *Complete Degree Course Offers*, published by Trotman, is among the directories which lists standard offers with this 'health warning':

> Institutions may raise or lower the level of published offers depending either on the quality or otherwise of individual applications or the numbers of applications received; grades/points offered may be adjusted downwards after A-level results. The level of an offer is not indicative of the quality of a course.

History Review regularly carries assessments of individual history degrees and comparisons between them.

University prospectuses and course-specific literature   Prospectuses and course-specific leaflets generally show students enjoying themselves, their faces animated and laughing; any frowns can be put down to deep thought. The images are, if not posed, selected, like the text, to give the best impression possible of the institution and its setting.

Open days and interviews   It is worth investing the time and money required to visit the universities and colleges on your shortlist.

Few admissions tutors interview candidates approaching through the standard A level or Access course routes. If you have been out of education for some time, contact the university or department to see if a consultative interview can be arranged.

Applicants who hold firm or conditional offers are generally invited to an open day. Like the prospectus, the open day programme has been designed to persuade you as a prospective student that this is the course for you. Leave yourself time to explore the campus on your own and, if you can, talk to students you come across during your reconnaissance – as well as to the 'trusties' the university or college has selected to act as guides. If you make your way to the office of the University Careers Service, you should be able to pick up a copy of the signpost sheet 'Your degree in history ... what next', published by the Association of Graduate Careers Advisory Services.

3
Sources and resources
Mary Abbott

Sources

Sources: see 'Documents"

Today, this definition, taken from the index of a book on the historian's craft published in 1971, would be considered excessively narrow. Documents remain the historian's core source but most practitioners would now acknowledge the contribution which the spoken word, images and artefacts should and can make to our understanding of the past. The range of source materials available to historians is, in consequence, potentially almost limitless.

As the bibliographies in older books make clear, historians habitually divide their sources into two broad categories: primary and secondary sources. Primary material is, in the strictest definition, first-hand evidence – though it should by no means be uncritically accepted as unbiased. Secondary sources are at one or more further removes from the actuality. The boundary between 'primary' and 'secondary' is very often blurred, and material in manuscript is frequently – and not necessarily appropriately – accorded a higher status than, for example, a printed book of the same date. Practitioners today often prefer a sequence which avoids the crude binary divide and reflects instead the location of manuscripts and, for printed material, the standard library classifications and the period being investigated. Anne Digby, whose study *Making a Medical Living, 1720–1910* was published by Cambridge University Press in 1994, classified the material she used as follows:

- manuscripts arranged by archive, in alphabetical order
- parliamentary papers
- periodicals and newspapers
- printed books and articles published in or before 1910 – *the terminus of her study*
- printed books and articles published after 1910

Of course the nature and volume of the historian's sources and the skills required to make effective use of them vary substantially with the topic and in accordance with the task upon which the individual is engaged. The materials used by historians working on superficially similar topics often differ substantially. If you set out to examine Nelson's contribution to the British victory in the Battle of Trafalgar, you would concentrate your attention on the surviving logs and journals kept on board ships involved in the action. The British material is identified in the *Report of the Admiralty Commission to Inquire into Tactics of Trafalgar* which was compiled by two admirals and the then Regius Professor of History in the University of Oxford, with the help of the Admiralty Librarian. If, on the other hand, you were working on the national response to Nelson's death you would explore a wider range of materials which might include state papers; private letters and diaries; the press; theatre posters; commemorative wares manufactured in enamel, glass, pottery, paper and textiles as well as in precious metal; the campaigns to raise funds to erect monuments – including a number of columns – to his memory. Most of the miscellaneous material listed here would qualify as primary.

The nature and volume of evidence and the skills required of you as an interpreter are not only dependent on the topic being investigated; they are also a reflection of the stage which you have reached in your experience or practice as an historian.

Most universities and colleges encourage, and many require, students reading for a degree in history to demonstrate an ability to work both on a broad canvas and in depth; to attempt to pose and answer questions about big issues – but even when they are conducting research in a very narrow field, few practitioners can hope to verify every scrap of evidence on the topic they are investigating. In consequence, historians are constantly obliged to depend on the work of their predecessors. We must, however, strive to be not passive receivers but constantly vigilant, critical clients. Historians' sources are inherently unreliable.

In most university history departments, the bulk of the undergraduates' diet is likely to be in the form of printed texts written or edited in the past decade or two. It is a commonplace that the makers of our sources, the historical actors, were prisoners of their rank, gender and values. So, to a degree not always sufficiently recognised by their students, are the professional historians who interpret them for colleagues, students and lay readers.

A good historian is a sceptic who takes nothing at face-value, is ever open to new ideas and is prepared to modify her views in the light of fresh evidence or persuasive argument. Few people now see history as a good predictor of future events. What history offers you is a chance to observe and analyse at second – very often at third or fourth – hand, the whole gamut of human behaviours, including our species' remarkable capacity for deception. This is a salutary experience and an opportunity to develop valuable transferable skills which you can make use of in the real world.

According to the task or, perhaps more accurately, the stage of the task on which you are engaged, you will approach your sources as investigator, judge, juror or advocate. Indeed, you will frequently assume each of these mantles in turn. The order in which these roles are listed, though not invariable, is not accidental. It mirrors the process of data collection, evaluation and argument in which the student engages in the course of preparing an essay or, indeed, a more substantial project such as a dissertation.

Whatever the volume, nature or classification of the historian's sources, the essential questions remain constant:

- who made the source?
- when?
- why?
- what accounts for its preservation?
- is it genuine?
- has it been tampered with?
- is it corroborated by other pieces of evidence?
- how scrupulously has it been interpreted by oneself, another student or practitioner, or the purveyor of hearsay in the past?

In most university departments the acquisition of the full range of technical skills which enables an historian to

- understand
- assess

- put into context
- interpret

complex historical data is normally the business of the postgraduate.

Thus as a first-year undergraduate writing an essay in response to a question on witchcraft in New England in the seventeenth century, you might use four, five or six chapters or articles recommended by your tutor. In the course of your undergraduate career, as you develop the skills and independence expected of a history graduate, you will be required to read more widely and more deeply, tackling monographs (specialised and authoritative book-length studies) as well as papers published in learned journals. Work on an undergraduate dissertation would almost certainly involve you in using primary sources directly and intensively but not necessarily in manuscript form. David Hall, author of *Witch-hunting in Seventeenth-century New England: a Documentary History, 1638–1692*, published by North Eastern University Press in 1991, reckoned that a close professional study of the topic demanded engagement with:

- primary – manuscript – material in the state archives of Massachusetts and Connecticut; in the university libraries of Harvard and Brown; the public libraries of Boston and New York and the Essex Institute at Salem (although David Hall takes this for granted, a prerequisite for work on these archives is the ability to decipher the often difficult handwriting of the period)
- editions of seventeenth-century documents printed between 1850 and 1975
- a critical evaluation of commentaries on witchcraft and religion in Europe and the English colonies in North America in the sixteenth and seventeenth centuries
- a familiarity with the laws and legal processes of the States
- an evaluation of the interpretations of witchcraft put forward by anthropologists, psychologists, sociologists and students of gender

As a graduate student you would grapple with a similar range of source materials; your topic would be more narrowly defined.

Resources

Students should recognise that university and college libraries (or learning resources centres, as some institutions now label them in acknowledgement that their holdings include electronically stored images, text and sound as well as printed paper) offer, in addition to books and periodicals, invaluable assistance in the form of works of reference and expert staff.

The libraries available to history undergraduates range from the great copyright libraries like the Bodleian in Oxford or Cambridge University Library (CUL), to the small focused collections held by colleges which may teach no more than the equivalent of the first year of an undergraduate programme. Cambridge University Library's stock of books, journals, dissertations, maps, music, audio-visual and other materials is listed in seventeen separate catalogues. Much of the library's stock is neither relevant nor accessible to undergraduates.

CUL uses an idiosyncratic system of classification in which the date, subject and *size* of a work all have a part to play. Most libraries have adopted the Dewey Decimal classification which assigns the numbers between 900 and 999 to history – with interruptions for geography at 910 and biography at 920. But history books are widely distributed – so that, for instance, family history is classified with other material on the family and sits on the sociology shelves at 306.85 and the history of trade unions is shelved with other material on unions (331.88) on the shelves assigned to economics. Thus, in the course of their undergraduate careers, history students are likely to find books on their reading lists located in the sections formally designated as anthropology, economics, geography, history of art, literature, politics, sociology and science.

If you routinely consult the larger-scale general and the specialist dictionaries held in the library you will enlarge the number of words and concepts you understand. The very brief definitions contained in the pocket dictionaries are sometimes misleading. If you were reading about the Reformation of the sixteenth century and consulted a very small dictionary you might might encounter a definition of 'humanist' as 'an individual who does not subscribe to any religious doctrine but sets out to live according to ethical principles' – a puzzling description to apply to Erasmus or John Calvin. The multi-volume *Oxford English Dictionary* (*OED*), by contrast, offers a series of meanings, among them a reference to the scholars who pioneered the study of the language, literature and antiquities of Greece and Rome. The interpretation of documents from the past is complicated by the tendency of the meanings of words to shift. A sexual encounter might be described as 'naughty' in texts written three hundred years apart – in the 1690s and the 1990s. To appreciate the gravity of the charge in 1696, you would probably have to consult a more experienced reader or a large-scale dictionary: in the sixteenth or seventeenth century 'naughty' meant 'morally bad or wicked'. In a similar way, today 'nondescript' means 'ordinary'. Two hundred years ago, as readers of Patrick O'Brian's novels will be aware, 'a nondescript' was an exotic plant or animal, never before described by naturalists. Dictionaries arranged on historical principles, like the *OED*, are museums of words.

You will find that compendia of historical facts, like the series published by Macmillan and written by Chris Cook and a series of colleagues, are invaluable quick-reference aids. The volume covering the years 1760 to 1830 includes among its many helpful tables and sections lists of archbishops and bishops, members of governments, the franchise in English boroughs before the Great Reform Act of 1832: in Cambridge the voters were the freemen of the borough; in Reading resident male householders paying the poor rate, and in Northampton the male householders not in receipt of poor relief – the 'pot wallopers', as they are often known. The list of new Knights of the Bath includes Arthur Wellesley, the Duke of Wellington, honoured in August 1804; the duke's entry in the section 'Biographical details of major commanders' provides a potted biography.

As a student of English history you will benefit from the great monuments to the energy of the Victorians: the *Dictionary of National Biography (DNB)* and the *Victoria County Histories (VCH)*. The *Dictionary* is currently being updated to reflect the developments in scholarship and values in the intervening period. Many more women and many more men without an 'Establishment' background will be included in the *New Dictionary*. Work continues on *VCH* .

Atlases provide you with evidence of physical geography – for most of human history mountains were barriers, rivers were arteries along which goods and passengers travelled, sea-goers were dependent on favourable winds. Historical atlases supply graphic commentaries on the histories of population, economics, religious change and the causes and results of conflict. Like tables of statistics, maps tend to look, to the naive eye, like definitive statements of facts. They are, of course, the product of a process of selection and interpretation, to be used, like all the historian's sources and resources, with sceptical care.

4
Note making
Mary Abbott

History students make notes on source material – still primarily texts –
lectures and discussions. This chapter examines:

- reasons for making notes
- the characteristics of effective notes
- strategies for note making
- formats

The characteristics of effective notes are described under the heading
Essentials. You have many more **Options** when it comes to strategies
and formats.

Why make notes?

Acquiring good note-making skills will help you develop as an active
and effective reader, listener and participant in discussion. In these con-
texts, notes are aids to:

- concentration
- comprehension
- memory

and enable you to

- express, organise and control information and ideas

Like many of the other skills you should acquire as an undergraduate historian, the ability to make effective notes is transferable into the rough old world of work.

Essentials

Notes made from sources must be:

- accurate
- easy to trace back to the source
- in your own words
- organised
- useful

Notes must be accurate because they are among the key components from which you construct

- written and oral assignments
- exam answers
- major projects and dissertations

Take particular care when transcribing

- technical vocabulary (words like bourgeoisie)
- proper names

Sloppiness will undermine your tutors' confidence in your work and distract them from appreciating its merits. (If you attend formal meetings of clubs and societies or sit as a student rep on a university committee you will be aware that the agenda requires members to scrutinise the minutes for accuracy before going on to consider matters arising and substantive issues.)

Notes must be easy to track back to their source because references, whether they appear in bibliographies or as foot- or endnotes, enable you, your tutors and your student colleagues to verify the evidence you have marshalled in support of your arguments.

Always record the:

- author
- title of the book, article and journal
- place and date of publication
- pages

on which your notes are based.

The widely used Harvard referencing system is described on pp. 49–50. Although you will not include it in your reference, a note of the Dewey or other catalogue numbers of the texts you have consulted often saves time in the long run.

If you are making notes on pictures or artefacts, whether in the permanent collections of museums or galleries or in temporary exhibitions, the label and/or catalogue entry will provide the necessary data. If your subject is a church or a house open to the public, record its location and, if it is in the care of a trust or society, identify its custodian.

Notes must be in your own words this:

- protects you from the vice of plagiarism (see p. 44), which tutors penalise severely
- enables you to assess your understanding of the material you are working on. Until you can express an argument or a theory in your own words, you can't be confident that you have grasped it. Rephrasing helps you to understand and assimilate the meaning of the sources you are working on.

Notes must be organised effectively because it is a waste of time recording information and ideas unless you can retrieve them. You must be in a position to find and manipulate the material you have recorded. Beware of the dangers of losing control of the boundaries between the notes taken from different sources and your own critical response to evidence and argument. That said, how you organise your notes is up to you. It is considered under the heading 'Options' later in this chapter.

Notes must be useful because, unless they are fit for the purpose for which you have made them, you will have invested your time in vain. Just as a skilled minute-taker omits irrelevant discussion, so the skilled student will produce notes geared to the task in hand. An all-purpose precis of a text is rarely called for. **Select** and **connect** must be your watchwords.

Because you are selecting relevant material, **notes should normally be significantly shorter than the text on which they are based.** There are exceptions: particularly dense passages of argument may require a lot of unpacking. But, if you decide that it is worth extracting a long quotation or a complicated table, photocopying will save time and prevent errors of transcription.

Options

This section of the chapter focuses on **strategies** and **format**.

Strategies

Note-making strategies vary by context and from student to student.

Books, chapters from books and articles are probably the easiest sources to handle because you can set your own pace and work within your individual span of concentration. It is much easier to get the gist of an argument if you read it straight through without pausing to make notes. At the same time, you can avoid a second read-through if you keep a note of the pages which looked particularly promising, together with a prompt to remind you of the reason for revisiting them. Well-chosen prompts will help you to organise your notes when you are ready to make them.

Lectures are trickier. So much depends on the lecturer. A synopsis of the lecture, circulated as a handout, written up on the black or white board or projected on a screen, will help you to identify the key points. Vocal emphases and gestures are also important clues. But even when you can recognise the important points, the difficulty of dividing your attention between listening and understanding the current point while making notes on the previous one remains. The best advice is to do your homework. If there is a prescribed text for your course, read it before you go to the lecture. In the absence of a prescribed text, use your initiative. In the last resort go to an encyclopaedia to equip yourself with the basic facts, concepts and vocabulary which provide a framework for understanding. However well or badly briefed you feel, try to set aside a few minutes before you go to the lecture to tune into the topic.

Lean lecture notes are generally the best. (In an ideal world you would be able to set aside time to 'flesh them out' after the lecture.) But it takes courage to listen while other people all round you are scribbling away. If you can, collaborate with other students, taking turns to listen with concentration and to commit as much as possible to paper, until you reckon you have got the balance between listening and recording right.

Seminar and tutorial discussions probably present the greatest challenges for the note-maker. The less structured the discussion, the harder it is. Again the sort of preparation suggested for lectures – together with

your lecture notes – will help equip you to identify significant new information and ideas. The bonus is that you have the chance, during or after the class, to ask contributors to elaborate their arguments and supply you with references. But remember the main purpose of these meetings is an exchange of ideas. As Chapter 7, 'Classes', emphasises, in a 50
seminar your pen should be on the table more often than it is in your hand.

Format

This is a matter for personal choice. So long as you follow the guidance outlined in this chapter and make sure that you can understand what you have noted when you come back to it after an interval, format is up to you. Traditionally, students have used ring binder and record cards. Notebooks and pads are obviously less flexible means of storage but, if you are inclined to lose or confuse loose sheets or cards, you may find a sense of security in a series of well-indexed notebooks. Personal Computers (PCs) are new and potentially very powerful environments for storage and retrieval.

There are other choices to be made too – between, for example, lined and plain paper. Think about the ways in which you draw attention to the points you consider important: underlining, boxing, block capitals, highlighting with a fluorescent pen are among the options. Some people are happier with notes which are staccato or telegraphic versions of continuous prose but it is worth experimenting with other non-linear patterns – mind maps or spray diagrams, as they are sometimes called, especially when you are playing about with ideas and the connections between them. Be conscious of the danger of letting presentation distract you from the substance of your notes.

Endnote

Just to indicate how the storage and retrieval of information has changed since the beginning of the century and to ram home some of the points I have made in this chapter, let me quote from Reginald Lane Poole's obituary of Lord Acton, which was published in the *English Historical Review* of October 1902:

He has been credited with a marvellous memory, and this certainly came out conspicuously in his conversation. But his power of citing the appropriate text was artificially assisted by the habit which he early formed of making written extracts of whatever struck him in his reading. These selections, made on slips of paper of a uniform size, were arranged and classified and stored in a prodigious series of boxes and drawers. On the advantages of such a method it is unnecessary to insist, and many laborious students may well envy the ease and security with which Lord Acton compressed the cream of his reading into compartments and was able to produce it at demand.

5
Essay writing
Mary Abbott

The academic essay

History essays have a great deal in common with the essays required of students of other disciplines in the humanities and social sciences. The questions humanities and social science students are invited to address normally relate to issues which, if not controversial in the everyday sense, are open to more than one interpretation and, therefore, debatable. The most significant variations affect what we might think of as the beginning and end of the process of producing an essay and have to do with the nature of their core sources and the different conventions governing presentation. This chapter deals, first, with the generic strategies for producing a satisfactory academic essay and then with the defining characteristics of the good history essay.

Why write essays?

It is important to explode the myth that essays are a burden imposed on students by sadistic tutors as a kind of initiation rite. Essays enable you as a student (as well as your tutors) to test your understanding, judgement and application. They provide your tutor with opportunities to make the constructive comments which should enable you to work towards more successful performances in future essays and thus, since essays are still the prime means of assessing the achievement of students of the humanities and social sciences, to enhance the status of your final award. Although very few graduates will be required to write academic essays in the world of work, the skills developed in the process of essay writing are skills which are demanded in almost every kind of career or profession to which a humanities/social sciences graduate is likely to aspire: diligence, judgement, controlled imagination, the capacity to persuade, which of course implies good communication skills.

The process of essay writing

Submitting an essay to your tutor is best thought of as the end stage of a complex, intellectually demanding and time-consuming process which involves a number of linked elements, principally:

- investigation
- evaluation
- decoding the question
- constructing an academic argument in response to the question
- drafting
- editing

and, finally,

- presentation

Except for the final stages, the order is not immutable. There is often a strong academic case for undertaking the investigation or, as students often tag it, the 'research' for an essay before focusing down on a specific question. Pressure of time or, for instance, the need to get through an unpalatable but compulsory task can push 'decoding the question' to the head of the student's agenda.

Pacing yourself

Given that so few students are keen examinees, it is puzzling that so many claim that they can only write essays when they are working against the clock with the adrenalin flowing. This way of working is unwise. Whatever the habits of their youth, tutors, in their judicial capacity, act on the formal premise that students work steadily through the term or semester. Thus, if a crisis blows up at the last moment and a short-term illness or other emergency prevents the submission of essays by the expected deadline, any extension you are granted is likely to reflect this assumption.

Investigation

Students almost invariably receive guidance in the form of a list of set or recommended reading. It is worth investing time in analysis of the booklist: any discernible bias in the reading list will provide clues about your tutor's own perspectives on the topics under review. At the same time, competition for books and lack of time prevent students from consulting every item recommended by their tutors. Indeed, it is not necessarily desirable that they should. You should, however, have a clear and conscious strategy to guide your reading. Most academic essays require students to examine controversial issues. A recent general survey will frequently provide you with grounding in the subject and an outline of the views and composition of rival schools of academics. Thus briefed, you are ready to dig deeper and tackle the specialist literature in the form of books, chapters from books, articles in learned journals (giving due attention to the range of interpretations), and whatever raw materials are relevant to the topic.

It is generally a good practice to begin by skim reading material. At this stage, full notes are rarely a sound investment but do take the time to mark your trail, recording the pages you want to return to with a word or short phrase to remind you of what caught your attention.

As you read and reread, make it your practice to note ideas as well as facts. Always make sure that you can trace your notes back to source. Be scrupulous in your use of references and quotation marks to distinguish the words you have copied from your commentary on them. **Plagiarism – the theft of other people's original research, ideas or expressions – is regarded as a serious academic crime and, if detected, is likely to be severely punished.**

Note-taking styles vary from person to person and it is worth experimenting until you find the format and the method of storage that suit you best. A few general points are worth making: space your notes out so that you can add points and ideas. According to the size of your wallet and your preference, you may keep your notes on sheets of A4 paper in a ring binder; on a set of record cards stored in a box or secured with a rubber band; in an electronically elastic file held on a hard or floppy disk.

Avoid being tempted into too condensed a record: you need to be able to make sense of your notes when you return to them after a gap. At the same time, notes should be significantly shorter than the text on which they are based. It is worth making a photocopy of dense text, tables and similar data and using a highlighter pen to pick out the key figures and phrases.

Evaluation

Investigation and evaluation are, of course, intimately linked. Students who engage with their material naturally weigh up the evidence and the ways in which it has been interpreted as they go along. But, at least once in the process of developing an essay, the time will come to stand back and take careful stock of the material you have accumulated. We say 'at least once' because, having reviewed the situation, you may find that you need to take steps to fill in gaps you have identified.

You must, however, curb any tendency towards the inhibiting variety of perfectionism that prevents students meeting deadlines. Even if you find it frustrating, it is vital that you get into the habit of doing the best job you can in the time available to you. This is among the most important skills a student can acquire.

Decoding the question

There are good reasons for investing time in decoding the questions set by your tutors. Tutors invariably mark down work which lacks focus. For students working within the constraints of word limits, the penalties for irrelevance are especially severe. Translating the question into your own words is a useful way of testing whether or not you have grasped its meaning. Decoding the question also helps to expose gaps in your knowledge and understanding, and thus leads you to revisit the evidence. As a bonus, the process of analysis often provides you with a possible structure for your response.

Essay titles generally include a command:

- assess
- criticise
- discuss
- evaluate
- review

Every one of these imperatives could be replaced by the instruction: 'exercise your judgement'. The unwritten coda is 'and persuade me that your position is tenable'; in other words, 'argue your case'.

Constructing an academic argument in response to the question

The planning stage is one which students skimp at their peril. There is a strong case for investing the time necessary to produce a plan detailed enough to free all your energies for the vital and demanding task of expressing your argument clearly when you translate your plan into continuous prose.

Whether or not you opt for this solution, it helps to break your task up into easy stages. First concentrate on constructing the argument. Leave the introduction and conclusion until later.

It is worth noting that academic arguments rarely conclude with a clear-cut verdict. Historians, in particular, seldom have a water-tight case. There is almost always too much bias and too many gaps in our evidence. Lack of certainty fuels historical debates. It is one of the things which makes history enjoyable.

There is no single winning formula for a successful academic argument. But, bearing in mind that the academic essay is normally a critical discussion of a controversial aspect of the topic you are studying, it is possible to identify a small repertoire of strategies for presenting the pros and cons. The line you decide to argue will influence your choice.

Perhaps the most common – and safest – approach is to put both (or all) sides of the debate even-handedly, systematically assessing their strengths and weaknesses, and concluding that there is something to be said for each of the opposing positions. If you are in strong agreement or disagreement with the proposition embodied in the question, and have the evidence and theoretical reasons to make your case, the arguments in support of your conviction may justifiably occupy the bulk of the space available. Even in this situation, it is essential to invest some words in demolishing the opposing viewpoint. A very well-briefed and confident student may sometimes choose to attack the question itself. This bold approach *can* pay dividends: tutors who appreciate free-thinking students are likely to reward an energetic and well-founded assault on the question but the response of less open-minded tutors may be less than generous.

The way in which you present your plan on paper (or screen) is a matter of personal preference. Many students feel most comfortable working towards a series of headings written one beneath the other. Experts on study skills, by contrast, often advocate an approach which produces a plan resembling the trunk, branches and twigs of a tree or a spider's web. This strategy certainly makes it easy to slot in additional points. And, when it is used successfully, it produces a plan which can represent (and test) the cumulative strength of an argument in a strikingly graphic way. It is well worth experimenting to see which way of working suits you best.

Drafting

Like any other person who writes for a living – the journalist, the publishing academic, the romantic novelist, the advertising copywriter – the student is well advised to consider her target readership. As a student, the ideal reader you should have in mind is not your tutor but a fellow student or you yourself as you were before you started the course or module on which you are now being assessed: interested, intelligent and sceptical, but a novice in this particular field. To put it another way, you should not assume expert knowledge of the topic or discount what you have learned from lectures and discussions in class.

It would, however, be a mistake to lose sight of your tutor entirely. Shrewd students soon become skilled judges of their tutors' characters. Is this tutor invariably eager to promote debate, open to ideas? Or do students get their heads bitten off if they challenge the view set forth in lectures? Most tutors sit somewhere between the two extremes.

It is hard to be self-critical when you are struggling to meet a deadline: get into the habit of managing your time so that you can return to your draft after a few days to review the structure of your argument and the clarity of your expression with a fresh eye. Since you will rarely be completely satisfied with your first shots, it is worth drafting your essay on a computer or word processor, if at all possible, and using its capacity to cut, insert and rejig text, thus avoiding the need for a total rewrite and, very probably, a final copying up 'in neat'.

Presentation

The spell check not only enables you to correct misspellings and 'typos' but also provides incidental entertainment: the common surname Harrison, for example, is not recognised by the spell check on the Apple Mac which offers as alternatives: 'Harris', 'harpoon', 'harridan' and, as an outside possibility, 'horizon'; the less common Yarwell is interpreted as a possible attempt at 'earwax' or 'earwig'. In addition, the word processor enables even the least skilled 'two-finger typist' to produce a professional-looking text. This is not a trivial bonus: there is little doubt that the appearance of your essays will influence the marks you are awarded. An experiment carried out by the Open University some years ago demonstrated that a sample of tutors consistently scored a neat typescript more highly than an untidy manuscript even when the content was identical. And fairly so – arguments which are easy to grasp are awarded higher marks than those which are difficult to follow: signposting and legibility each have a part to play.

And so, if you've come into higher education without the skills of word processing, don't begrudge the time put in to acquire them. They will prove their worth during your career as an undergraduate and make a useful contribution to your CV when you are ready to look for employment. In some institutions IT is a compulsory part of a skills programme for students at the beginning of their course.

Editing

This is your chance to step out of the writer's role and look at the argument and supporting evidence through the eyes of your imaginary ideal reader – responsive and open-minded but alert and critical. Is the case before you persuasive? Do the links in the chain of argument bear the weight of the conclusion? Is the discussion easy to follow? (If you drive, you'll know how frustrating poor signposting can be.) Acquire and use a vocabulary of signposting words to emphasise your key points and indicate what you plan to do next:

- *for instance* introduces evidence
- *similarly* introduces corroboration
- *but*, *however*, *on the other hand* all introduce qualifications to the case you are presenting
- *thus*, *in consequence* signal that you are winding up a section of your argument

The finished product

- introductions
- conclusions
- bibliographies

Introductions

The introduction is the place to explain why you have tackled the question the way you have: why, for instance, you have stressed some points at the expense of others.

We recommend that you model yourself on the journalist rather than the writer of a whodunit and summarise your argument in your introduction rather than leaving the denouement to the end. The main justification for this strategy is that your tutors, who will almost always be marking under pressure, need all the help you can give them to ensure that they take in every jot and tittle of your argument and the evidence you have marshalled to support it.

The introduction is a topic on which tutors' prejudices vary – the advice we give reflects our own. If your tutors have different ideas, it might be wise to go along with them.

Conclusions

The first and the essential job of the conclusion is to remind your reader that you have done what was asked of you. You have considered the proposition, weighed up the evidence and – usually – come to no very definite conclusion.

But the conclusion provides the confident and well-informed student with a chance to end up with a flourish, to open the question up and thus to suggest that, given the opportunity, she could develop the argument to embrace a wider time scale or a bigger geographical area.

Bibliographies

Titles cited in the body of an essay

The titles of books and journals should be underlined or *italicised*. The titles of journal articles should be put inside 'quotation marks'.

References in the body of an essay

Preferences may vary from department to department but, unless contrary guidance is offered, we would recommend the 'author-date' or, the 'Harvard system', as it is often called: Abbott (1993) p. 39 indicates a direct quotation; Abbott (1993) pp. 172–186 refers the reader to the source of an argument.

Bibliography

Every essay should include as an appendix a bibliography listing in alphabetical order all the books, articles and any other sources you have consulted. If you are using the Harvard system in the body of your essay, entries should give the following information in the following order.

Books Entries:

- author's surname: Abbott
- author's given name or initials: Mary *or* M.
- the date of publication: (1993) in round brackets
- the title: <u>Family Ties: English Families, 1540–1920,</u> underlined or, if you are using a word processor, in italics, *Family Ties: English Families, 1540–1920*
- the publisher and/or place of publication: Routledge, London *or* Routledge *or* London – be consistent in your practice

Articles For articles in journals the format produces entries like this:

Hindle, Steve (1994) 'The Shaming of Margaret Knowsley: Gossip, Gender and the Experience of Authority in Early Modern England', *Continuity and Change* 9(3): 1–20 – that is volume 9, part 3 (probably the autumn issue), pages 1–20.

Essays For essays in edited collections, the format is:

Pollard, John (1990) 'Conservative Catholics and Italian Fascism: the Clericofascists', in *Fascists and Conservatives: the Radical Right and the Establishment in Twentieth-century Europe*, ed. Blinkhorn, Martin (London), pp. 12–49.

The history essay

The criteria outlined above are necessary but not sufficient to produce a good history essay. The writer of a history essay must demonstrate, in addition, a sound understanding of the historical context of the ideas, developments or events under consideration: to put this at its simplest, the historian needs to indicate where the topic being discussed is located in time and space. This may mean commenting on the physical environment; beliefs and values; social, economic and political structures and institutions; the technologies of the period in question.

In contextualising, the writer of a history essay must recognise that hindsight is a dubious benefit. To assume that outcomes were inevitable is a grave mistake. Partisanship is to be avoided. Your personal sympathies with those whose opportunities, civil rights or material circumstances were adversely affected by race, rank or gender must not be allowed to colour your evaluation. A good student aims for clinical objectivity; a partisan produces polemic.

As the chapter on sources makes clear, an educated scepticism is the hallmark of the historian. And yet, well-founded speculation may not be out of place. Indeed, it is an element in the hard-to-pinpoint quality of originality or flair which lifts work into the First Class.

Although professional historians who contribute to radio and television frequently speak in the historic present – 'It is 1837, the young queen Victoria has just ascended the throne . . .' essays should be written in the past tense.

Feedback

Normally feedback or assessment comes in at least two varieties: marks and comments.

Marks awarded to undergraduate essays – and to other kinds of formally assessed work – are banded into classes: First, Second (generally subdivided into Upper Second ('Two-One') and Lower Second ('Two-Two')) and Third. The marks which differentiate the classes are as follows: First 70–100; Upper Second 60–69; Lower Second 50–59; Third 40–49.

Work awarded fewer than 39 marks has failed to achieve Honours standard.

'Pass' or 'Ordinary' degrees are awarded to students who opt not to complete the Final Honours stage of a degree programme. They are also granted to students who have narrowly failed to achieve the standard required for Honours.

There is general agreement about the characteristics associated with First, Two-One, Two-Two and Third Class performance in the humanities and social sciences.

First Class work

In the humanities and social sciences marks of 80 or above are used very sparingly indeed. Any mark of 70 or above is regarded as outstanding. First Class work is characterised by some, or all, of the following qualities:

- penetrating analysis
- wide and adventurous reading
- a sophisticated grasp of issues
- a confident command of context
- originality
- cogent, cumulative argument, fully supported and documented
- fluent written style

Upper Second Class work

Upper Second Class work is characterised by some First Class qualities but they are displayed only intermittently. Work of this class is very good but not outstanding. It is marked by some, or all, of the following qualities:

- good analysis
- thorough familiarity with a wide range of the relevant literature
- a sound grasp of context
- a good focus on the question
- a developed argument
- an array of detailed, relevant evidence
- a good level of literacy

Lower Second Class work

A Lower Second is not a bare pass. Work in this class is good. It is characterised by some, or all, of the following characteristics:

- adequate analysis
- dependence on a restricted range of reading
- a limited understanding of context
- a good but incomplete answer to the question
- an adequate argument
- a patchy array of evidence
- an adequate written style

Third Class work

Third Class Work is weak but of Honours standard. It demonstrates some, or all, of the following characteristics:

- limited analysis
- limited reading
- a poor understanding of context
- a lack of focus on the question
- a weak argument
- inadequate evidence
- poor use of English

Failed work

Students fail for a variety of reasons. A mark of zero is normally only awarded to students who fail to submit an essay; a mark in the high 30s indicates that the writer is close to the threshold of the Honours pass.

Many students, especially those at the beginning of their undergraduate career, are performing well below their true potential. Their work may well combine some of the characteristics of a First Class answer – wide and adventurous reading, perhaps – with some of the characteristics of a Third – a lack of focus on the question. Students working towards a better class of performance benefit from the often painful process of reading their tutors' critical comments carefully and taking them to heart.

6
Examinations

Adrian Gregory

Much of the advice which applies to essay and dissertation writing also applies to exams. It's a good idea to read or reread the chapter on essay writing alongside this one.

What is the point of exams?

What is the point of exams? Many people dread them and even good examinees doubt whether they are the best way of testing the student's skills, knowledge and understanding. It may comfort you to know that lecturers have asked themselves this question and much less weight is placed on exams now than used to be the case. The way in which work is assessed and, in particular, the balance between exams and continuous assessment varies from institution to institution. This may well be a factor which influences your UCAS choice. It may be possible to find a place which will enable you to achieve a history degree without taking any exams at all. Nevertheless, timed exercises still play an important place in most university schemes of assessment and the purpose of this chapter is to explain, first of all, why this is so and, second, to equip you to improve your exam performance.

The case for exams

Although it may come as a surprise to some of you, there is a very good case to be made for exams. The examination system was originally devised in the interests of fairness: in the nineteenth century exams replaced patronage and purchase as the means of selecting candidates for the Civil Service and officers for the Army. In consequence the senior civil servants who ran the Indian Empire in the second half of Queen Victoria's reign included the sons of gamekeepers, butchers and bakers, tailors and shoemakers, upholsterers and undertakers. Benjamin Jowett, Master of Balliol, who owed his academic career to his success as an examinee – his father was a printer – regarded exams as a character test. Advocating competitive entry to the Indian Civil Service, he wrote:

> For the moral character of candidates, I should trust partly to the examination itself. University experience abundantly shows that in more than nineteen cases out of twenty, men of attainments are also men of character. The perseverance and self-discipline necessary for the acquirement of any considerable amount of knowledge are a great security that a young man has not led a dissolute life.

Many of the same considerations still apply today. There is growing concern in universities about the danger of electronic plagiarism: work done under exam conditions is demonstrably the product of the candidate's own unaided effort. The tutor's likes and dislikes are less likely to influence the marks he (or she) gives an anonymous exam script. Jowett's comments hold good: exams do test your capacity to keep calm, to work under pressure and think on your toes – abilities which are important in the rough old world of paid employment. This is what the political sketch writer, Matthew Parris, a journalist not uncritical of ministerial performances, wrote of the Scottish Secretary in October 1995:

> Mr Forsyth listens to the question, thinks on his feet, then gets properly to grips with it. . . .
> He leaps at the Dispatch Box, confident of his intellectual mastery, unafraid of what anyone may throw at him, because he understands his own argument. He speaks in a coiled, measured, very slightly menacing way, as though dictating.
> Hansard reporters will need little work on a Forsyth answer: the phrasing, the grammar, the balance of subordinate clauses – almost the punctuation – are all there.

In other words, his performance at the Dispatch Box has all the hallmarks of a 'good examinee'.

And don't forget that exams can save you time, a very precious commodity for those of you with family responsibilities, part-time jobs or other outside commitments – sport, theatre, student journalism.

Exam formats

As we've already pointed out, exams have changed since Jowett's day. In recent years some tutors have been thinking hard about the ways in which they assess their students, designing methods to fit the particular range of knowledge, skills and understanding which they are seeking to develop in students taking a particular course or module As a result, undergraduate exams come in different shapes and sizes and, although it is not yet extinct, the traditional end-of-year three-hour marathon which requires you to tackle three or four unseen essay questions is no longer the dominant form. Many conventional essay-based exams are now shorter. In modular systems they may occur at the end of a term or the end of a semester. In other words, there will be exams three or two times a year. Other exams depart from the old model in more radical ways. You may be allowed to take set texts or other material into the examination hall. You may get advance warning of the question. If this happens, unless you have a photographic memory, do not attempt to write an essay in the usual less pressured way and learn it off by heart. You may find yourself sitting exams designed, for example, to test your understanding of political ideas by inviting you to comment on an extract from *Das Kapital* or your knowledge of the political geography of the Habsburg Empire by asking you to add the missing names of cities, states and rivers to a map of the world.

Preparing for exams

- making use of past papers
- active revision
- coping with stress

Whatever the format, the same general advice applies. Success in exams, as in other kinds of test, is most likely to be the reward of the canny candidate, who identifies and practises the essential techniques. Think of the amount of time and effort people put into practising for their driving test. The same principles apply to academic exams. Find out what is required of you. Practise. Don't wait until the last minute to revise. In some modular schemes there may be little or no time between the end of teaching and the start of the examination period. Even if there is a gap for revision, it is good practice to consolidate your knowledge and understanding as you go along.

Making use of past papers

Past papers *can't* be used to predict which topics the examiner will select. However, if they are used correctly, past papers are an invaluable asset to the exam candidate, so much so that, if there are no past papers, you should ask your tutors to provide a sample paper. When you use past papers, it is important to make yourself aware of the rubric – the local rules which apply to a particular exam – **how many and what sort of questions are you required 'to attempt'**, to use the classic and depressing language of the examiner. Check that the rubric isn't about to change. 'Failure to observe the rubric', doing too many questions or too few, muddling the regulations for sectionalised papers, may lead to the failure of an otherwise well-prepared candidate.

There are other good reasons for making yourself familiar with past papers. Papers set on an earlier occasion give a good idea of **the range and style of questions** you will face. If you are preparing yourself to sit a three-question paper, you should have a minimum of five topics you would be able to tackle.

Active revision

When you have chosen your topics, it is time to begin to gear yourself up for the exam. Reread your notes but don't sit hunched over your file. Make this an active process. Highlight or underline key facts (the names of the authorities you'll want to cite as well as, for instance, dates) and the key ideas. You may find it helpful to produce a condensed version of your notes on record cards.

Reading something new can help to freshen up your thinking – a book review from a broadsheet newspaper, the *Times Higher Education* or *Literary Supplement* or the *London* or *New York Review of Books* (all almost certainly available in your institution's library) won't take you long to get through and might pay big dividends in the form of new ideas and at least two names to drop into an exam answer: 'As Marks argued in his blistering review of Spencer's ... '. If you are confident that you know who your examiners will be and what their prejudices are, you can, of course, adjust your wording to suit. 'As Marks alleged in his blistering review of Spencer's otherwise well-received . . .' might go down better.

Back to the past papers yet again. If you collect all the questions on, say, Irish Home Rule set over a period of five or six years you can **test both your all-round knowledge and understanding of the topic and your ability to select what is relevant to a particular question**. The most effective way of doing this is by making answer plans. The challenge of making plans may expose gaps in your knowledge or understanding which you may need to plug. A student who can **plan a good response quickly** (by which I mean in five or six minutes) is at a tremendous advantage in an exam (and, as the example of Michael Forsyth suggests, this is a valuable asset in real life too). Brain storming and refining answer plans is one element of preparation which you can usefully do with other people who are facing up to the same exam. It *is* possible to have a good time gearing up for exams with friends and a jar of coffee, some cans or a bottle of wine.

Learning to get an argument down on paper within the given time allowance is another vitally important skill, one you have, in the end, to develop on your own. The irresolute might experiment with the strategy that concentrates slimmers' minds so well and agree to **practise writing to time** with a support group of equally weak-willed friends. If possible, get a tutor to comment on what you produce. Alternatively, discuss the essays with your friends in the 'support group'. Remember that university exams are not like the old 11+. You are not in direct competition with each other.

Bear in mind that tutors may penalise you quite severely if you fail to **complete all the questions you are required to attempt**. Compensation for an unfinished answer is – quite rightly – regarded as unfair to the candidates who have delivered what they were asked for in the time allowed.

Knowing how much you can get down **in legible handwriting** in, say, forty-five minutes will help you to scale your answer and allocate appropriate amounts of time to the different elements of the paper. **Illegible scripts irritate examiners**. If your handwriting is difficult to read, experiment with different instruments, try writing bigger, join a calligraphy class. If there are genuine physical reasons for your inability to write legibly, your university should be able to make appropriate special arrangements by giving you access to a keyboard or providing you with an amanuensis or scribe. Obviously, tutors have to have advance warning of any special needs.

Coping with stress

Many undergraduate have learned to fear exams by going through the A-level hoop. At this stage in your education, the grade you get may seem to you, your parents and friends to be desperately important. After all, it's what will decide whether or not you go to Footlights College, Oxbridge. Except for the minority aiming for research funding, degree results are much less significant in the long run. The class of your degree will certainly matter a great deal at the time the results come out but, once you've been out in the rough old world for a little while, only the 'university bore' will ask you 'what you got'.

Of course, it pays to be sensible in the build-up to exams. Get into the habit of going to bed and getting up at conventional times and the thought of a 9 o'clock exam won't be quite so daunting. Drink less alcohol – you won't give your best performance with a hangover. If you smoke, remember that you'll have to go without for the duration of the exam and condition yourself to appropriate gaps between cigarettes.

For some students, fear of exams is so ingrained and acute that it is worth their while seeking professional help within the university. Personal tutors should be able to point you in the direction of someone skilled in teaching stress management and relaxation techniques.

The exam itself

Try to get a good night's sleep. Revising all night won't help.

Once you get into the exam room, the crucial first step is to **read the whole of the exam paper carefully**. Take as long as you need. Mark the questions you might attempt but don't start writing immediately. Students tend to waste time trying to read the examiner's mind before they have seen the paper but skimp the time they devote to reading it when they have it in front of them. Often an exam question is an invitation to discuss a well-known historian's views. You may be given a direct quotation followed by the instruction 'Discuss'. It is good practice for the examiner to identify the source of a quotation but you will be rewarded if you are able to demonstrate a knowledge of the writer in question in your answer. Sometimes the question will refer to the title of a book from the reading list, even the key text: 'Was mid-Victorian Britain an age of reform?'; 'Did the twentieth century see the rise of a professional society?'. You will score marks if you spot the reference.

If you are required to answer more than one question, **begin by writing plans for both or all of them**. Remember that the best essays are the best-planned essays. You may find it helpful to start by jotting down as many points as you can think of but, of course, be prepared to discard everything that isn't strictly relevant to the question. It is better to end up with an answer that is well focused but on the short side than one which is obviously padded out with irrelevant material.

A coherent argument, clearly expressed and well supported, will stand out from the scripts cobbled together in a panic.

Evidence that you have thought for yourself will impress.

Sketch maps and diagrams may help to explain complex arguments.

Don't allow yourself to be distracted from your commitment to **relevance**. Confront the question head-on. Whatever happens, don't change your mind part-way through.

Show what you know. Dates and relevant accurate statistics look good. So do direct references to the historians you have read. At least as important is to **demonstrate a real grasp of the issues and an ability to put them in context**. **Avoid anachronistic moral judgements**. Reconstructing the thinking of the seventeenth-century witch hunter or the nineteenth-century trade unionist is an important part of the historian's trade.

Begin with an **introduction** setting out the key points in your **argument**. Just like their candidates, examiners are working under pressure and need all the help you can give them in following your argument.

End with a **conclusion**. Your conclusion may be **a firm 'yes'**, **a firm 'no'** or – as often as not – **a firm 'maybe'**. The conclusion is the ideal place for a final flourish. Take the opportunity to suggest that there are other, and potentially more interesting, angles on the topic, demonstrating that you have read or thought about related issues which you have not been invited to address on this occasion. Now is your chance to use the best of the ideas you had to discard at the planning stage.

Between the introduction and the conclusion comes the argument. There are three basic approaches: the two most common build up to the historian's usual firm 'yes' or 'no' or 'maybe'.

'Strong assertion' is a more pretentious way of describing the firm 'yes' or 'no'. If you take this line, you will concentrate on marshalling evidence and theoretical reasons in support of your contention. Either way, you will need to make at least a passing reference to the opposing point of view, if only to demonstrate why you have concluded that it is absurd. Usually, you will need to spend time on the demolition job.

'The classic dialectic' is a more pretentious translation of the firm 'maybe'. You put the case for both sides fairly, pointing out the strengths and weaknesses. You probably end up sitting on the fence. Or, if you are able, you may come up with an alternative conclusion of your own.

The third and by far the riskiest approach is to question the question. For this strategy to succeed, you need to be able to demonstrate that you have understood the question and could, if you wanted, provide a conventional argument – rather like an artist who can produce highly competent representational works but chooses not to. To adopt this strategy, you need to be confident that you have 'star quality'.

Whatever the pressure, resist the temptation to adopt what we might call the 'Blue Peter' strategy and produce an answer you prepared pearlier. The odds against it precisely fitting a question your tutors have devised makes the National Lottery look like a racing certainty. And try to avoid being reduced to incoherence. The result is the intellectual equivalent of what Barry Humphries used to describe as the 'technicolor yawn' – spewing up all you can remember about the topic in a thoroughly messy way. If you find yourself seized by panic in the middle of an exam, it may help to stop writing, put your pen down and look out of the window to the world outside the exam room until you calm down again. After all, there are more important things than exams.

7
Classes: preparation and participation

Susan O'Brien

As a history student you will find your timetables made up of lectures and classes, no matter what modules or courses you take. The classes are usually labelled 'seminar', although they may also be called tutorial or workshop or 'small group work'. New staff and new students soon learn that a range of pleasures (or tortures – depending on your experience) take place under the umbrella heading 'seminar'. Even the group size of this 'small-group activity' varies from university to university and course to course – anything between eight and twenty-five students being described in the same way. Although the group's size has an impact on the way the seminar works, there is no need here – or at any time – to become distracted by definitions or labels. It's much more important to understand what purposes your department, or course, or tutor intends from the sessions. Then you will be in a position to make the most of them.

Despite the variety of labels and activities, what distinguishes the class or seminar is its focus on **student participation.** Classes exist to enable you to engage in discussion with the tutor and, crucially, with one another. Your teaching staff, even those who gain great personal satisfaction from lecturing and believe it to be a valuable method of teaching, would agree that the seminar has much greater potential for you. Such potential is by no means always realised for reasons which will be analysed, explicitly and implicitly, in this chapter.

The purpose of this chapter is to enable you to get the most out of this form of teaching and learning. Looked at in purely economic terms, it is the most expensive form of learning you will undertake, more costly than lectures or individual study time spent in the library or elsewhere. Looked at another way, if you raise your own standards and effectiveness in a seminar you will inevitably lift the seminar for everyone else **because effective seminar participation is collaborative rather than individual**. This is what in the language of politics and business is called 'win-win', and you don't have to be a goody two-shoes to achieve it. Much more to the point is to be **purposeful** and **instrumental.**

Seminar activities

All of the following can take place under the heading of class or seminar. Please note my list is indicative not exclusive:

- a presentation by one student followed by a discussion
- short presentations by several students
- a group presentation
- a discussion, in which everyone is expected to participate, of particular questions and themes known in advance
- working in pairs or small sub-groups on particular questions, followed by a plenary session to share and focus on conclusions
- working together to understand and interpret documents, statistics, maps or other materials
- a debate, the group divided into two to defend or oppose a proposition
- the pursuit of questions in a less structured format

Why seminars?

I want to take some time over this because students, perhaps history students in particular, often regard classes or seminars as less vital than lectures. Or, more accurately, it takes them longer to learn the value of seminars. Lectures give you 'the stuff' to take away and, you hope, prepare for examinations and other assessments. What do seminars or tutorials 'give' you?

Students often say how much they would have benefited from more explanation about what tutors hoped for and expected from class sessions. They wish, with the benefit of hindsight, that someone had made explicit 'the rules of the game' and the thinking behind them. Tutors often think they have done so, but have a tendency to underestimate the need both to take time over this at the beginning of the programme – and to come back to it periodically. On the other hand, there is a movement in higher education towards making these 'rules' much clearer to students. The assessment of quality in teaching conducted by the Higher Education Funding Council is playing an important part in shifting higher education culture towards clarity and explicitness and away from mystery and implicitness. You can see this most clearly when you look at the changes to assessment. Many tutors now state in writing the criteria for assessment, informing students about what is expected. Such a movement is rather less evident in the area of teaching and learning methods. Not all academics will agree that it always helps to be explicit, but it is difficult to see why you should take several terms or semesters to stumble into understanding (and possibly never fully achieve it) when you can be told from the outset why historians (and others) so value the seminar.

The seminar or class has the potential to be:

● flexible
● responsive – or at least more responsive to *your* interests and thinking about a subject
● active
● an exchange of ideas, knowledge, perspective

We all learn constantly through the exchange of ideas, knowledge and values in conversation. Whether we are talking about the latest film, a sports fixture or an item of current news, we are finding out about the subject of the conversation, ourselves and other people. What takes place in a seminar is a 'conversation' of sorts, but one which is formal, structured, artificial and controlled. Even though it doesn't precisely mirror any setting you will meet in other walks of life, it can help you enormously with many situations you are likely to encounter. Why is this and how can it help?

It does so because of the **values** intrinsic to the 'class' approach to learning and because of the **skills** it enables you to develop and practise. Many contemporary study guide-books will emphasise the skills aspect of this learning, but we would miss something essential to our study of the humanities if we overlook or ignore the values.

Let's look at the **skills** first. A class or seminar allows you to develop and practise a range of skills. Make your own list of these before looking at the list below:

- attentive and purposeful listening
- intelligent questioning
- formally presenting material or an argument 'live' rather than simply in writing
- developing your argument and defending it
- thinking 'on your feet'
- critically appraising the argument and evidence put forward by yourself and others
- experiencing group dynamics and improving your understanding of them
- playing a range of roles within a group: leadership, supporting, challenging, ice-breaking, etc.
- problem-solving in a group

Not all types of class allow you to develop a particular skill to the same extent, but across the range of your courses you will have plenty of opportunity to develop in all the areas listed above.

What about the **values** I claimed underlie the very existence of this approach to learning? Think about this for a moment and jot down your own list. My list comprises:

- tolerance and respect for the views of others: in this structured environment it is not in the 'rules of the game' to interrupt, shout, fall asleep, chat to your neighbour, or walk out
- open-mindedness and fairness: as part of the 'rules of the game' we have to weigh up all views expressed, make a critical judgement, and be prepared to have our own ideas challenged
- recognition that there is often more than one perspective or interpretation: human experience is multi-dimensional, not readily reduced to formulae; we might wish there was a single, simple answer but have to recognise that human experience is more complex

We need to add to this list (and your own) the fact that seminars also allow us to explore **values** through discussion – who thinks this and why? I hope you can see more easily why this form of learning can play an important part in our development as historians and, more importantly, as intellectual and moral beings.

Now compare what you and I have said about the purposes and processes of 'classes' with the statement made by the Council for Industry and Higher Education in its 1990 document 'Towards a Partnership: The Humanities for the Working World':

'We are not looking for knowledge in our recruits. We are looking for mastery of the processes by which knowledge can be acquired and a maturity and sympathy gained from exposure to the mainstream of intellectual thought' (Robert Reid, Chairman of Shell UK Ltd).

. . . The most important function of higher education is to inspire its students with a passionate inquisitiveness to continue learning through life. The humanities have a central role in redefining and transmitting a common culture of objectivity, tolerance, judgement by relevant evidence and fairness. . . . Even within a single discipline, the humanities strongly emphasise the capacity to see a thing from several perspectives at once. 'It is the mark of a genius', F. Scott Fitzgerald wrote, 'to be able to hold two contradictory ideas in the mind at the same time.' In a world of abundant ambiguities and uncertainties, this is a valuable business attribute too. . . .

Recruiters from companies in all sectors tell us that one of the principal qualities they seek is the ability to work well in a team. Many management development programmes feature multi-disciplinary teamwork and the capacity to motivate others often figures prominently in criteria for promotion.

Employers of humanities graduates agree that interpreting demanding texts, distinguishing fact from assertion, and appraising doubtful arguments offer a training in critical power and lucid expression. . . . Business particularly values among its managers those who can stand back from the pressure of immediate opinions and alluring trends. Persuasive skills have their place but so does the ability to see through them.

Values and skills are so closely connected in this document that it is not particularly fruitful to try and separate them out. Instead, it is worth noting that the attributes desired by those who wish to be 'well educated' in the humanities sense of the word, are also desired in business and industry (and, one might add, anywhere – including at home). And only a cursory analysis serves to inform us that these attributes must be developed and honed in dialogue and working with others.

All very fine but, you might legitimately ask, does it help me with the short-term and pressing goals of **passing assessments**? If asked to say which will most help you to answer the questions in examinations and assessments – lectures or classes – your tutors will say that seminars win every time. In seminars you are rehearsing the very processes which go into answering questions and solving problems: framing the possible responses, weighing the evidence, considering alternative interpretations, coming to conclusions.

The better your **preparation and participation,** the greater your chance of realising the potential of the seminar.

Preparation

The challenge of talking about history

I want to begin by acknowledging some of the challenges of history seminars. If the overall aspiration of the group is, to borrow Rostow's famous analysis of industrialisation, to 'take off into self-sustained growth', there are good reasons why some history seminars stay grounded. Leaving aside the possible explanation of poor teaching, part of the explanation lies in poor student preparation, and part in the intrinsic challenges of talking about history. Let's look at the latter first.

Getting a good exchange/discussion going about history is certainly challenging. There are particular difficulties not experienced to the same extent by other academic subjects. I don't offer this as an excuse but make it as an observation from experience, starting with my own and adding to it that of hundreds of other combined or joint Honours history students who have been in a position to make informed comparisons between their subjects. In literature, philosophy and theology there is often a text to analyse together or a significant theoretical approach to work over. In human geography many classes have a practical and problem-solving dimension, again working from materials together. Sociology, women's studies, communication and media studies draw to some degree on contemporary society and culture, enabling students to make use of observation and experience as well as reading. Art history focuses on analysis of the visual, and looking together can help group discussion.

Historians can – and do – make use of slides, maps, documents, artefacts and newspaper clippings. They can employ information technology. But, as history students know, these do not constitute the heart of the matter in most of their courses. Observation can be relevant (for example, observation of buildings and landscape) but it rarely is. Informed speculation or deduction can play only a limited part. Nor is personal experience of much help when you are studying the responses of backwoods farmers in the American Revolution, the nature of the family economy in fifteenth-century France, or the operation of British imperial policy in nineteenth-century West Africa. Indeed, backwards projection of our own contemporary attitudes is positively unhelpful. The women and men of the fifteenth century are emphatically *not* ourselves dressed in period costume so we can't simply deduce how they might have responded or what they experienced.

The upshot of all this is that, as a student of history, you can feel underwhelmed by how little you can bring to the discussion and overwhelmed by your own lack of hard knowledge of events or phenomena, and by the array of interpretations.

Moreover, the speed at which you move through historical periods can add to your discomfort. At school, and particularly at A level, students take a period and study it in great detail. You might spend several hours a week for six months on the Reformation as an A-level student, only to have it whiz by in three weeks of a first-level undergraduate module. My own first-year course in American history travelled from 1609 to 1968, leaving me with a residual feeling of anxiety throughout the seminars. Did I know who was President during the Civil War, let alone at any other time? What if anyone put me on the spot and actually asked me? Frozen and fearful, I endured the seminars, never believing I *knew enough* to make much contribution.

What can be done to face these very real challenges and to liberate yourself from those which merely cause unnecessary anxiety? What should *I* have done to increase my learning and my enjoyment?

I could start by simply recognising what the built-in challenges are and accept that it is not just me. The tutor knows this too. Next I can remind myself that I don't *have* to come to each session as a one-woman band, but can be part of a group who will tackle the questions together. Then I could try taking as much control as possible of the situation as an aid to building confidence and increasing my preparation and the time I spend on reading and thinking about the task. After all, I would not go on holiday without planning the itinerary, taking a good hard look at the possibilities and what I wanted to get out of it. (OK, so I admit it – I might just take a package holiday and lie in the sun. But you take the point, I trust.)

Take control – look ahead

● If the module has aims or learning outcomes, spend time familiarising yourself with them – the assessment will be closely linked to them

- read the course/module handbook from start to finish *before* the end of the first week; see the course whole from the start and keep the whole in mind
- pay particular attention to the nature of assessment and the nature/content of the classes/seminars
- work out what is being expected *and* what you hope to get from the course. Remember the holiday analogy. If you are on a rapid tour of European cities you expect to get a glimpse of each. Rome in a day is not the same as Rome for the week, although both are likely to include St Peter's and the Trevi fountain
- check out the library for resource strengths and weaknesses; possibly work out which assessment interests you most

Take control – practical planning

- Convert all your modules into diary form, marking in lecture titles, seminar topics and seminar preparation periods
- if you are responsible for a session (e.g. a presentation or chairing), mark this in and mark in the additional preparation time
- mark in the date when the assignment is due or the examination is scheduled, and sketch in the preparation time
- plan your use of the books and articles for the assignment by reserving them, copying articles, or reading and note taking ahead

Even if you are unable to keep to these plans, you will have a framework within which to deviate and tack about, according to need and reality. The first two weeks of a new course can often be slow while the last two weeks are frenetic. You can even this out to some extent by anticipation and planning.

Participation

What I have to say about this is strongly influenced by my belief that learning in classes is not a competitive but a collaborative endeavour. It's not about getting 'one-up' in some pecking order, but about learning. History tutors don't usually spend much time on the group dynamic angle of the seminar and you won't be assessed on it. Nonetheless, the dynamic will play a significant part in your experience.

Being a member of the group

- the tutor does have control, but you are an adult participant
- make an effort to know and use the names of fellow students (your tutor should supply a list if you ask for everyone to have one)
- think about the group dynamics as the weeks go on
- rearrange the furniture if necessary – it can make or mar a discussion
- let the tutor know any problems: you both have a great deal to gain

Two common worries

Shyness   It may be that several weeks have gone by and you haven't felt able to make any contribution even though you have been well prepared. Many tutors periodically build into the classes chances for small groups of three or four to discuss a topic and this is often a real help in confidence building. But what can you do if this isn't the format and wish you could join in? One possibility is to see the tutor out of the seminar time and just tell him or her that you find it difficult. Your tutor will probably ask if there is any approach that would help you (e.g. making an opening for you to ask a question, asking you a question directly, getting people to work in pairs and report back, ignoring you until you feel ready). If you can manage it, you'll find it very helpful to take this approach. Other alternatives are to talk to your personal tutor, the study skills tutor or your year tutor.

Try writing down a question before each class and look for an opportunity to ask it. A prepared question has the merit of being written down and gives you the chance simply to practise saying something.

Always remember that you are likely to over-estimate everyone else and under-estimate yourself. What's more, you are very likely to over-estimate what the tutor is expecting. Believe me when I say that tutors are aware when someone speaks for the first time and will be wanting to encourage you.

Taking notes in seminars   Note taking should not be your main activity in a seminar but many people spend a lot of time doing it. Everyone wants to make the most of any good points that are made. But people also often hide behind note taking, or do it compulsively. This is the time for thinking and for engaging in discussion – just make enough notes to jog your memory. The basic posture in a seminar or class is to have your pen on the table and not in your hand. Limit yourself to headings, or a diagram approach. The main structure of the discussion and the major points are all that you need to take down. This is definitely not the occasion for capturing factual information. If you are worried about not having notes, ask your tutor for five minutes before the seminar ends when he or she can draw it to a conclusion and draw out the main points that have been made – so that everyone can take notes.

Let's pick up again on the skills you will be using in the seminar and **prepare for specific aspects of seminar participation**.

1 Purposeful listening

Listening is greatly undervalued as a skill, possibly because it appears to be passive. But attentive and purposeful listening is an *activity*. Listening in this way requires interest, concentration, the ability to put aside one's own preoccupations for the moment, and be open-minded. Interestingly, comprehension and engagement are not determined by the degree of fluency of the speaker. In fact, the fluency of the tutor can sometimes be a positive hindrance, as he or she flows on, enthused by his/her own ideas. The more hesitant contributions of other students can often be more useful for you to use as a measure of your own comprehension. The basic rule is to listen as you would wish to be listened to: with respect and an imaginative sympathy.

Good listening is linked to astute question asking and to useful interventions.

2 Question asking – asking questions of the tutor or one another

Questions *can* be asked during and after lectures. But we all know the blocks involved here. Questions in seminars can be for straightforward checking of your understanding ('Have I got this right?') or for pushing your understanding further ('If Countryman says xxxx about the origins of the American Revolution, then how can Fleigelman have argued xxxx?'). The role of curiosity is a vital one in the development of historical understanding – but also of understanding more generally. It is also one of the main ways human beings have of showing an interest – in a topic and in one another.

Question asking may seem very straightforward but, as you know, it simply does not come easily. Many tutors invite you to take up questions from the most recent lecture or from readings. The response is often a dead silence until one member dutifully dredges up a question, largely, one suspects, to rescue the poor tutor. Question asking can be greatly improved by preparation and anticipation. You *know* this opportunity will come up and that it is valuable. Look at why you don't make more use of it. Is it poor organisation? (Where is that question you scribbled down in the lecture? Or as you were reading?) Or fear of appearing too ingratiating? Or lack of confidence and a fear that the question will be seen as revealing the stupidity of which you suspect yourself, but no one else?

Poor organisation   There are many ways to improve your organisation. Use yellow stick-it labels in your file; write questions in coloured felt-tip; have a coloured sheet at the back of your file and jot questions down as they occur.

Fear of appearing ingratiating   Yes, so if you keep asking questions perhaps your fellow students and tutor may think you are overdoing it. If this is likely, then it is a matter of disciplining yourself and learning to read other people's body language. This is a useful thing to do anyway.

Fear of appearing stupid   This is the most common fear and the least likely to be realised. Almost everyone feels the same and the tutor knows it. Remember that the most obvious seeming questions are not. Remember also that the tutor will be able to use any question to good advantage for the class, building on it. And remember that most tutors are so glad that you've asked and given them an opener that, even if the question could have been better expressed, they will be able to work with it. Abandon this fear as soon as you can by trying out, in true 'Blue Peter' fashion,4

one you have prepared earlier. Get used to hearing your own voice out there and then keep practising.

3 Responding to the tutor's questions

Just as your questions can have different important purposes, so can those of the tutor. She may be checking up to see whether you have understood or she may be pushing on your thinking and opening up a new line of discussion and analysis.

Responding to questions is more familiar than asking. It is something that we have all had to do in school and we don't have to take the initiative, which makes it easier. But our responses can often be stunted. It takes practice to develop an answer which can lead the session forward beyond 'the answer'. Perhaps your response can end with a further question, or invite others to comment. Don't worry about this. It really is a matter of practice and having patience with yourself.

4 Making a presentation

One of the most common formats for the seminar is the student presentation. If you dread the idea of it you will most certainly share this feeling with almost everyone else in the group. Even people who talk readily at home or in a group of friends can become awkward and tongue-tied when put into the more formal setting of a seminar (or a job interview, or a presentation at work, or chairing a meeting). These occasions require each of us to 'perform' or to take on a role, and the skills can be learned. Presenting a seminar will help you with all these formal performances.

Before you start to read and make notes spend a little time thinking about the overall purpose of the presentation, and your overall approach. Make a list of the features of a good seminar, from your experience as a listener. It might include the following:

- it keeps to the time limit
- it has a pace which allows easy listening
- it provides an overview of the topic first – it does not go straight into detail
- it uses quite short sentences and gives 'signals' such as 'my first point'
- it gives a handout which summarises main points
- it uses visual material
- it raises questions for the group to discuss
- it informs you of the sources used

Notice that these features show a high level of awareness about the listener – and less concern for detail and high level of content. A seminar is not another mini-lecture but a chance for discussion of big ideas or main arguments. If you provide too much detail, these aspects may be lost. So, take courage. It's not a waste of time to think about effective communication as well as content.

Assume, for **example**, that you have been asked to give a presentation of ten minutes' duration in your first-term module on 'Industrialisation in Britain 1740–1830'. The topic is 'The "Consumer Revolution" 1740–1780'.

You know that the purpose of the presentation is to provide the basis for discussion, a 'kick-start' for the remainder of the session. You don't need to provide all the material, only a number of pointers for discussion and some conclusions of your own to provoke interest.

The reading list is pretty long and you don't know which books or articles are best. Start with your course textbook (John Rule's *The Vital Century: England's Developing Economy, 1714–1815*) which has a good summary of about ten pages. This shows you that there is a debate among historians about whether a consumer revolution took place and, if so, when it started. *Here is one of the points for discussion.* You read around this for a bit more evidence. Rule also points you to the question about who was able to afford to buy consumer goods and in what parts of the country. *Perhaps this might make a second area for discussion, although at this stage you're not sure how different it is from the first.* Several of the sources he uses are also on your book list and look as though they will help with fleshing out what consumer goods people were buying in the eighteenth century. *Here is another dimension for the presentation.* You read McKendrick and parts of the huge *Consumption and the World of Goods* edited by John Brewer and Roy Porter. There are some excellent illustrations in the latter and you decide to photocopy a few to pass round. By now you can see how easy it would be to get carried away with the idea of a consumer revolution – the paintings and engravings of markets, and of piles of Wedgwood pottery, newspapers and magazines, books and clothes, tempt you into making strong statements about this phenomenon. But you recognise the need to stay open-minded, so you pull back and ask a question instead: how important was this consumption to the economic growth in England during the period? *This gives you a fourth area to raise* and that seems plenty. You develop your presentation round the following:

● the historical debate about whether there was a consumer revolution: you are quite interested in the fact that a good many of the books on your list date from the 1980s and you want to make the

point that the consumer decade of the 1980s seems to have added a good deal to the debate
- the nature of consumption in the period: what was the range of goods and why that particular range of goods?
- the question of who did the consuming and the extent to which regions differed
- the importance of home demand as a factor in economic growth. Was it crucial? How did it compare with foreign demand? Or with other factors?

The presentation can be structured as a brief discussion of these areas and you can raise a question, with your own thoughts for each. You will indicate at the start that there are four areas to your presentation and write up the names of your sources on the white board. The illustrations will serve as an ice-breaker for discussion as well as underlining your points.

What about your script? It helps to write very clearly, and large enough for you to follow your own notes easily. This also helps with nerves. You could use a separate large record card for each of the four points and write a heading with sufficient notes to talk from. Or you could script every single word. Do what makes you comfortable, but practise different approaches as time goes on.

How do you handle questions? This is another valuable skill to develop. Some people don't like the idea of having to answer any question that may come up because they won't have a chance to look anything up or think for very long about it. If you need time to think, try repeating the question, writing it up on the board, or asking the person to clarify it if necessary. You are not expected to be an instant expert and if you don't know it is best to say so. But you can invite anyone else to contribute and see if you can broaden out the participation. When you do answer, try to look around the group and not just at the tutor or the person who asked the question. This also broadens out the discussion.

5 Taking part in a discussion

When we talk to friends we have many small signals to help the conversation to flow. If we want to know something we can simply say 'What did you think about ...?' or volunteer an opinion as a way of getting a response. We use all kinds of 'conversational glues' – the 'ers', 'ums' and 'you knows' of conversation, to keep things going and encourage them along. A seminar is formal, even where it is relaxed, and we are not freewheeling in the same way. It might help you to know that academics have stock phrases or gambits that are designed as 'discussion signals' too. Here are some you might find useful to try (note how helpful it is to know names): 'When Joanne was talking about xxxx, I wondered whether xxxx'; 'Can we go back that point we were discussing earlier when . . .'; 'In the lecture, we were told xxxx. But I don't see how xxxx'; 'One of the things that puzzled me/interested me was . . .'; 'From what I've read about it, I don't see how we can say that . . .'.

My guess is that you will find these kinds of 'links' artificial and a bit of a strain at first. They are artificial. But so are many of the ways we operate through talk. Think of formal meetings with their 'Matters arising', 'Any other business' and the need to talk to other people round the table through the chairperson. Or think of Parliament and the rules it uses for debate. Or the meeting of any society, club or group you belong to. There are ways of getting into the conversation in all of these, and ways of killing the debate or keeping it alive. The aim of all the gambits I've suggested is to keep it alive by pushing the discussion further.

Some students (and tutors) measure the success of a seminar by the degree of heat generated; and, indeed, strong discussion can be stimulating and enjoyable. But in history seminars much more is likely to be achieved if a wide range of evidence and a number of different interpretations can be weighed and judged even-handedly.

Conclusion

You have several years to practise all the skills outlined in this chapter and to try out different approaches. What seems like an ordeal at first will get easier, and can become a source of pleasure as you realise how much you have learned – not only as a historian but as a communicator.

8
Research methods
Kim Reynolds

A piece of research is now a component of many undergraduate courses in history, either as an option or as a compulsory element. Specific requirements differ, as does the terminology used to describe the exercise: dissertation, project, research essay, thesis. But the consistent aim is to give you an opportunity, usually in your final year, to use your critical and creative talents independently. The dissertation differs in a number of ways from the kinds of work you have previously undertaken. The novel challenges of an undergraduate dissertation include:

- independence
- tackling new sources
- scale
- presentation

And all this has to be achieved within the framework of institutional **regulations**.

Independence

Your dissertation, unlike taught courses, does not come as a ready-made package. You will be given some guidance on your choice of topic and will have access to an academic supervisor. You may also take a course to prepare you for research. But responsibility for planning and carrying out the project is your own. You will have to draw up your own bibliography, decide which questions you want to ask and work out a strategy for completing the project by the given deadline.

Tackling new sources

You will work with new sources, going beyond the works of other historians to look at documents, texts or artefacts generated in the period which you are investigating. Using these sources, probably for the first time, might well involve you in using unfamiliar libraries and other resource centres – County Record Offices, for example.

Scale

Your dissertation will be an extended piece of written work, two or three times longer than an essay.

Presentation

The presentation of a dissertation is at the heart of the exercise. In particular, you will be required to provide the full foot- or endnote references to your sources and a complete bibliography of your reading. Together these make up the 'scholarly apparatus' of a work of historical research. Your finished work will be typed or word-processed and bound. You must ensure that it is grammatical, well punctuated and free of typing errors and spelling mistakes. In short, your dissertation should resemble a well-produced book.

Regulations

The specific requirements for dissertations vary from university to university. Before you launch yourself into research, make sure that you know exactly what is expected of you. You will not get any credit for following the regulations but you will be penalised for ignoring them. It is vital to check up on:

● permitted length – does this include the scholarly apparatus?
● amount and nature of the help you can expect from your supervisor
● regulation format
● deadline for submission

Formulating a research topic

The time spent in formulating the questions you want to ask, finding your materials and planning your research will pay dividends. Research is most effective when it is focused on a clearly specified topic. A vague feeling that you would like to do something on Nazi Germany or witch-craft or the history of your own town is only the starting point.

Intellectual frameworks for formulating a topic

All dissertations need to be related to the wider historical context but there are, essentially, two styles of dissertation: **source-led** and **problem-led**.

Source-led topics

If you choose to write a source-led dissertation, you will engage with a collection of correspondence, a run of a newspaper, a set of artefacts – family portraits, for example. The danger of source-led dissertations is that researchers may get so carried away by their enthusiasm for the material that they present it without analysis, without reflection and merely for its own sake. Historians call this magpie-like tendency 'anti-quarianism'.

Problem-led topics

Problem-led topics start with an issue debated by historians, which you seek to answer, through an analysis of evidence which is not necessarily archival.

Practical considerations

- scope
- time available
- access to sources
- languages
- other skills

Scope

You may well have to narrow your subject to fit the word limit and give yourself a chance to study your chosen theme in depth. A narrow topic can be as intellectually challenging as a broad one.

Time available

At the most you will have a summer vacation and most of the following academic year to complete your dissertation. Much of your time will be taken up by other academic work and your routine out-of-college commitments. Don't under-estimate how long it will take you to design your project and allow time to write it up and present it properly.

Access to sources

Choose a subject for which the sources are available locally. (And by 'locally', I mean where you spend most of your time. Don't assume that you can do enough research for a viable project on a three-week trip to Boston or Berlin. If your home is in Newcastle and you are studying in Bristol, you will need to calculate whether you are better placed to make use of sources in the north-east or the south-west.) If you can't get local access to sources, consider a problem-led dissertation.

Languages

If you are considering a dissertation on a region where English is not spoken, you need to decide whether you are able to read the appropriate language well enough. Alternatively, choose an angle which enables you to concentrate on material in English. For example, if you want to study the Spanish Civil War but have little or no Spanish, you might consider looking at the way the war was reported in the British press or at the role of English-speakers in the International Brigade.

Other skills

The same reservation is true of other skills – quantitative methods, database design, interviewing techniques and palaeography (reading medieval script).

Careful definition of your topic will protect you from the worst of all possible situations which is to embark on research only to discover that the topic is unmanageable and you have to begin again from scratch.

Practical guidelines for success in research

Follow the down-to-earth advice in the next three sections and you will be well on the way to producing a satisfactory dissertation.

- sources and resources
- research strategy
- writing up

Sources and resources

In writing your dissertation you will need to use what historians call primary and secondary sources – in other words, contemporary evidence and subsequent commentaries and opinion. A simple example would contrast a letter from Charles I appointing a friend to a political office (primary) with Linda Levy Peck's book, *Court Corruption in Early Stuart England* (1990) (secondary).

Primary sources provide you with the contemporary evidence on which to base your arguments. They do not have to be handwritten documents. If you are studying the passage of the 1833 Factory Act, your principal primary source might well be Hansard's record of parliamentary debates and the parliamentary papers relating to the Act, all of which are in print. And if your subject is architectural history or the history of the development of a town, the buildings and street plans might well be your most important sources.

However rich your sources, you must not neglect the commentaries which create the context for your argument.

Where to find your sources

Before you make a final decision about your subject, you must make a thorough investigation of the materials available to you. Most libraries operate an inter-library loan service which enables readers to use books from other libraries. This is extremely useful but it can be time-consuming (books can take months to arrive) and expensive (many libraries now charge for this service): find out what your library's policy is and be wary of relying too heavily on inter-library loans.

Most university towns have public libraries which often have holdings of books, journals and newspapers. Don't be put off by all those dog-eared paperbacks: many public libraries have extensive reference sections. They can be particularly useful if you are considering a locally based study, since many of them have runs of local newspapers dating back over many years.

Some libraries have local studies collections which concentrate on materials relating to the area. County Record Offices are the repositories of local archives: many produce leaflets outlining their collections. If there are other universities or colleges in your locality, find out what their holdings are like and whether you might be able to use them. If you plan to work on artefacts rather than texts, you will want to explore the local museums and art galleries.

Finding aids

There are many tools to help you identify the materials for your dissertation.

Library catalogues Finding materials has been made much easier by the introduction of electronic catalogues. The beauty of electronic catalogues is that you can use them to search in a variety of ways, unlike paper catalogues which usually require you to know the name of the author and the title of the book. Use subject searches to find out the titles of books in your area. Every time you come across something that might be useful make a point of recording the author, title, date of publication and shelfmark on a record card or in a notebook. If you notice that one shelfmark keeps cropping up, go to the shelf and scan it for related books. If an author has written one book on your field, check to see whether she has produced any others. If you can access catalogues of other libraries through a computer link-up, have a go. Remember that even if a book is not in your library, you may be able to get hold of it through inter-library loans.

Bibliographical works There is a whole industry devoted to the production of bibliographical subjects, listing – and sometimes commenting on – books and articles. They can be general, for example Lucy M. Brown and Ian R. Christie, *Bibliography of British History 1789–1851* (1977) or quite specific, for example K. D. White's *A Bibliography of Roman Agriculture* (1970). Bear in mind that works published after the bibliography will be missing. The Royal Historical Society publishes an *Annual Bibliography of British and Irish History* listing everything from Romano-British archaeology to twentieth-century social policy.

Abstracts *Historical Abstracts* and *Dissertation Abstracts International* come out several times a year. They are arranged by subject and contain brief statements about the content of books, articles and postgraduate theses. The abstract should be used as a finding tool, never as a substitute for reading the original work or as a means of padding out your bibliography. Examiners look for evidence that you have used the material you list.

Academic journals and literary reviews Academic journals and literary reviews provide a useful indication of how new books have been received by the scholarly world. If there is a journal which specialises in your area, keep an eye out for new issues – most come out three or four times a year. *The Times Literary Supplement* and the *London Review of Books* also carry reviews of books of interest to historians and often publish lively debates on historical subjects.

Books and articles As you read, you will come across references to other books and articles which might be worth following up. Footnotes and bibliographies are often rich quarries.

Archives The National Registry of Archives, Quality House, Quality Court, Chancery Lane, London, WC2A 1HP has an extensive record of archival resources.

Some do's and don'ts

- DO look beyond your college library
- DON'T just turn up at another library and expect to be able to use it
- DO talk to librarians and archivists: they are the experts on their collections and can be extremely helpful especially when they realise that their assistance is appreciated
- DO remember that books and articles can be ordered through inter-library loans – but don't forget that it can be a slow and expensive process
- DON'T spend so long identifying materials that you have no time to read or think about them

Research strategy

This section offers advice on time management and effective research techniques to make the time you invest in research as productive as possible.

Time management

There is no single formula which will provide everyone with an effective timetable but you should find these general guidelines useful.

Make a realistic assessment of the time you have at your disposal. Consider the following:

- how much of your vacation are you going to be able to spend on your project?
- how many other courses will you be taking and what are their assessment deadlines?
- how much of your social life are you prepared to give up?

Your supervisor will undoubtedly have a view on the appropriate amount of time a student should devote to a dissertation: this will sometimes be an unattainable ideal. You need to be practical as well as ambitious. There is no point in drawing up a timetable which presupposes that you will spend fifteen hours a week on your research if in fact you can only give it eight.

Set yourself some interim targets. Break the project down into sections: **definition of topic; location of sources; research; writing**.

Decide, for example, to have the topic defined before the summer vacation (you may well find that you're required to do this), the resources located and the preliminary reading done by the New Year, a draft written during the spring term and a final version completed over Easter.

To meet these targets, you should set yourself short-term goals: something to achieve week by week. If you find yourself failing to keep up with your timetable, ask yourself why. There are several possible answers: **your timetable is unrealistic; your project is over-ambitious – you may need to restrict it to a smaller selection of sources; you are spending too much time on preliminary tasks; you are not giving enough time to your dissertation**.

If you are running ahead of schedule, ask yourself whether you are being sufficiently rigorous in your research.

Preliminary bibliography

Set yourself a strict time limit for the preparation of your preliminary bibliography. Virtually any topic you can think of can produce a reading list of several hundred items on related themes and issues. You won't have time to read them all, so there is no point in searching feverishly for every last one. Be selective. Use *Historical Abstracts* and book reviews to decide which works are worth concentrating on for a start. As your project takes shape you will come across new material and, very likely, recognise that some of the items on your preliminary bibliography are irrelevant.

Recording information

Experience will teach you the method that suits you best. Whatever system you choose, keep it simple. And whatever system you choose, include the following points for every text you read:

- full name of author (both correspondents for letters)
- full title of book/article (that means the subtitle too)
- publisher of book and place of publication
- full title of journal
- date of publication (date of letter/manuscript, if available)
- library shelfmark (full reference of document, if available)

If you get into sloppy habits, you will find yourself spending the last few days before the deadline scrabbling around for these references for your footnotes and bibliography. This will prove enormously frustrating and will almost certainly induce a sense of panic. Similarly, when you transcribe a direct quotation, note the page numbers. If you don't, you will find yourself frantically thumbing through texts looking for references at the last minute.

If you use a computer, take the basic precaution of making backups and printing out regularly. If your machine crashes and you lose everything, you might get some sympathy, but without a dissertation you won't get an Honours degree.

Early drafts

It's a good idea to write up your material as you go along. It enables you to save and clarify ideas you might otherwise forget, it keeps the themes of your dissertation in your mind, and it may help you to identify the next stages for your research; it also exposes gaps in your knowledge and understanding. Most important, it means that, when you come to write up your dissertation, you won't be faced with a blank sheet of paper and a huge stack of notes. That scenario is extremely daunting.

Writing up

Writing is a very individual process and at this stage you should do what suits you best. But your dissertation will be of a quite different order of magnitude from the asssignments you have tackled at earlier stages in your undergraduate career. Even if you work best under pressure (the 2 a.m. essay writer), you must not leave this task to the last minute. Even if you were physically able to write the text, providing footnotes and bibliography, checking references and so on, it is a time-consuming business. Equally important, a dissertation is judged as a sustained piece of discussion, which weighs up every item of evidence and reaches a reasoned and considered conclusion. But keep a sense of proportion. Think of the dissertation as a series of closely connected essays, tackle one chapter at a time and you won't find the challenge impossible.

When you have written a complete draft, stop thinking about your dissertation. For a week or so concentrate on something completely different. When you come back to your dissertation with a fresh mind, you will find it easier to identify its strengths and weaknesses. With this fresh understanding, you should be able to revise your text effectively and – one hopes – with renewed enthusiasm. Leave yourself time to comb through for spelling mistakes and typing errors. If you use a word processor, the final stages will never involve a complete rewrite.

What your examiners are looking for

The consistent development of an argument   If there is no argument the dissertation is merely a collection of information. The argument needs to be free from contradictions.

The relevance of discussion   There is a strong temptation to include all the ideas that have occurred to you. Be tough with yourself. If it doesn't carry your argument forward, leave it out.

The appropriate use of evidence   An argument is only as good as the evidence you can muster to support it. Make sure your examiner can see where your evidence came from. If you spent hours gathering demographic data in a churchyard, make this clear, otherwise your examiner may assume you took it from another source. This is an opportunity to show off a bit.

The structure of your argument

Signal where your argument is going. If you can, persuade a (frank but supportive) friend to read your final draft and see whether she understands the messages you are trying get across. She needn't be a historian or even a student.

Presentation

A scruffy typescript will prejudice the examiner against you. Allow time for proofreading. If you are having your dissertation typed by someone else, allow time for retyping if it is not satisfactory. And make sure, before you commit yourself to any arrangement, that your typist understands that this is part of the deal, whether the work is being done for love or for money. If you are using a word processor, take the usual precautions and safeguard yourself against last-minute crashes and problems with printers. If you are using college equipment, don't leave things to the last moment or you are likely to find yourself at the end of a queue of anxious students in the same boat.

Scholarly apparatus

Full scholarly apparatus – a full acknowledgement of your sources and influences in the form of foot- or endnotes and bibliography – is one of the features which distinguishes a dissertation from an essay. (You will notice that the use of the footnote is itself a departure from the efficient shorthand Harvard author-date system recommended for essays.) The assumption is made that, unless otherwise stated, a conclusion, an interpretation, an idea, is the author's own. If you use another person's ideas without acknowledgement, you have committed an intellectual theft. Footnotes and bibliographical references are the currency in which you pay for scholarly conclusions and interpretations.

Footnotes and bibliographical entries also equip your examiners to judge for themselves the use you have made of your evidence and to test the strength of your conclusions. The references you give set the context for your argument: they can show the reader at a glance the kind of debates with which you engage, acting as a kind of shorthand for long and complicated historiographical controversies.

The mechanics of producing the scholarly apparatus cause unnecessary anxiety. If you follow the guidelines we have supplied, you will have everything you need at your fingertips. Take our advice and compile your notes and bibliography as you go along and you will be saved tedious and time-consuming tasks at the end.

What should you reference?

- direct quotation from any source
- paraphrase from any source (the author's ideas put into your words)
- statement or conclusion derived from evidence not quoted or paraphrased
- further substantiating evidence which you have no room or need to cite in full in the text
- sources of general background information – this will probably appear in your opening pages, setting out the current literature on the topic

References are not needed for

- statements of easily verified fact and common knowledge
- your own conclusion based on evidence in the text

Bibliographical entries   Your bibliography should be a complete and accurate account of what you have read, not what you think you should have read. Examiners are more impressed by the careful use of a short bibliography than by a long but poorly understood list. What's more, if you include an item which you have not read and which reaches conclusions which are different from yours, your examiners will assume – at best – that your footnotes are inaccurate.

Check your institution's regulations to see whether there is a required style. If you are not issued with formal guidelines, find a book which uses sources similar to your own and follow its example. Be consistent. Identify your sources fully. Check your bibliography to see that all the works cited in your footnotes appear there. The following examples contain the bare essentials – notice the difference between footnote and bibliographical references.

Book – footnote
William R. Taylor, *In Pursuit of Gotham: Culture and Commerce in New York* (1992), p. 73.

Book – bibliography
Taylor, William R. (1992) *In Pursuit of Gotham: Culture and Commerce in New York*, Oxford University Press, Oxford.

Article – footnote
James Burke, 'The New Model Army and the problems of siege warfare, 1648–1651', *Irish Historical Studies 27* (1990), p. 24.

Article – bibliography
Burke, James (1990) 'The New Model Army and the problems of siege warfare, 1648–1651', *Irish Historical Studies* 27: 1–29.

Newspaper – footnote
The Times, 14 June 1939, p. 4 cols a–c.

Newspaper – bibliography
The Times.

Manuscript – footnote
Harriet Sutherland to W. E. Gladstone, 25 May 1861, British Library Additional Manuscripts 44325, ff137–9.

Manuscripts – bibliography
Gladstone Papers, British Library.

Programme for research

Use this checklist to frame a calendar for your work.

1 Find out the formal requirements for your dissertation.
2 In discussion with a supervisor, decide on a general subject area.
3 Investigate the resources available.
4 Decide on the topic.
5 Prepare the initial bibliography.
6 Draw up a timetable.
7 Research and writing.
8 Draft completed.
9 Final version of text completed.
10 Bibliography and notes checked.
11 Printing/photocopying and binding.
12 Submission.

9
Quantification
Tony Kirby

Of all the skills addressed in this book, quantification is the one you'll probably find least immediately attractive, least accessible and – at first glance – least relevant to your everyday needs as a student. You have to hold your head up among your peers: and you have to impress whoever's marking your latest essay or exam paper. Identifying and using your sources, taking notes and communicating your ideas effectively both on paper and orally may seem a more obvious recipe for success. They are not unique to history as a discipline: and whether you've arrived at university from school, from an Access course or any other background you've probably already got a good idea of how to go about them, and so can refine and build on strengths you already have.

But statistics are different, simply because they seem to involve a degree of **technical** expertise that most students feel they don't possess. You may be one of the exceptions, in which case you can safely skip this chapter. But if you regard figures with the fear and loathing normally reserved for spiders in the bath, read on.

Fear of figures

Unless you happen to be living next to a supermarket that takes regular deliveries of tropical fruit, the odds are that the spider is completely harmless. And it's the same spider, or one of its sisters, who spins the intricate webs you may have admired on frosty mornings. There's both a lesson and a warning in this: statistics *are* harmless and treated properly they can help you to succeed as a historian (after all, an ecosystem without spiders would be rather unpleasant for us humans). But they can spin a web of their own. The web is a means to an end: for the spider to catch food, for the historian to lend an extra dimension in the attempt to capture that elusive entity, the past.

Your suspicion of statistics may have several causes, but I would guess the following are the most likely.

- They're associated with economic history, which isn't exactly flavour of the decade. More specifically, they're associated with a particularly unapproachable strain of the breed, the Rottweiler of the discipline, econometric history (sometimes domesticated as 'cliometrics') which may seem to be more concerned with intellectual gymnastics – such as 'counter-factuals' – than the 'real world'. Counter-factuals can be dismissed as a cause of worry straight away: they're simply a tarted-up version of the old question 'what if...?'. What if the Spanish Armada had succeeded? What if Hitler had invaded England in 1940? What if Khrushchev hadn't backed down in the 1962 Cuban Missile Crisis? The counter-factuals that concern econometricians are less immediately exciting: what would have happened if railways hadn't been developed? How would the agriculture of the southern United States have developed in the absence of a slave economy? How different would the twentieth-century British experience have been if late nineteenth-century entrepreneurs had taken different decisions from those they did? Unfortunately, unlike the essentially political questions posed above they can only be answered effectively through the construction of sophisticated 'models', of an economy with and without railways, for example.
- From this, it follows that if you don't have a good grounding in theoretical economics, you may start to feel yourself lost, especially when you find familiar terms such as 'rent' and 'capital' used in unfamiliar ways. Matters become even worse when graphs, algebraic notation, symbols and equations are used, as inevitably they have to be.
- Statistics are 'dry' and 'boring', unlike other sources – primary or secondary – which can excite you with their immediacy.
- They 'dehumanise' history and, by concentrating on things that can be measured, over-simplify the complexity of historical change and development.

So, the problems lie partly with the figures themselves, and partly in the way they're used by historians. We're really looking at two different – but related – things:

- **statistics as evidence** ('descriptive statistics'): the sort of thing that can be found in any textbook (e.g., population tables)
- **statistics as a tool of analysis**: the manipulation of figures using **quantitative methods**, typically to explore such things as the relationship between two variables (e.g., the pattern of landownership in an area plotted against the date of parliamentary enclosure), to measure dispersion around a mean (e.g., the size of nineteenth-century landed estates), or to identify an underlying trend (e.g., population growth)

For much of this chapter we're going to be primarily concerned with statistics in the first sense, partly because this is how you're most likely to run up against them, initially at least. However, as you will see, this easily shades into the second meaning, as the temptation to 'play with figures' is a strong one. But we shall not be going beyond simple arithmetic: I'm not going to attempt here any formal instruction in quantitative methods: to do so would take up all of this book. But I'll give some guidance at the end of the chapter if your appetite is whetted and you want to pursue the subject further.

Why bother with statistics?

You're going to find yourself up against one, other or both of the approaches I've just outlined sooner or later. Virtually all branches of the discipline – with the possible exception of intellectual history – use statistics to a greater or lesser extent. Some, such as historical demography, are essentially statistically based, and there are some 'set-piece' historical controversies (such as the perennial debate over living standards during the British Industrial Revolution) where quantitative evidence plays a crucial role, and an essay on the topic would justifiably be marked down if it didn't grapple with the evidence.

But there's a more important reason, which in some ways isn't a 'statistical' one at all. Sixty years ago, Sir John Clapham, the leading inter-war economic historian, argued that every historian needed to employ what he termed the 'statistical sense': 'the habit of asking in relation to any institution, policy, group or movement the questions: how large? how long? how often? how representative?'[1]

In other words – and this applies to anything you say or write as a historian – generalise away, but back up your generalisations with hard evidence.

You need another sense as well: the **critical** sense. You can't accept sources, primary or secondary, at their face-value. You are going to spend a lot of time, as a student, investigating historical controversies. Consequently, you'll start to see the strengths and weaknesses of particular arguments and the sources – usually literary – they're based on. But figures seem different. In my experience, most students, when they use them at all, tend to do so rather uncritically. Tables of industrial production or whatever are solemnly copied into essays – often in splendid isolation from the surrounding text – as evidently self-proving. Figures certainly carry a degree of precision, and an air of authority that the written word lacks. But 'there is a kind of alchemy about figures which transforms the most dubious materials into something pure and precious; hence the price of working with historical statistics is eternal vigilance.'[2] When using figures, or looking at how other historians have used them, you always need to ask yourself:

- how accurate are they?
- how representative are they?
- can we check them from other sources?
- are they 'real' figures, or extrapolated from another source?
- do they support the argument being put forward, or can they be interpreted differently?

Rather than addressing these questions directly, I'm going to adopt an indirect approach through two case studies. The first is an attempt to show how historians work with figures, because it's only by looking at some 'real' data that you can fully appreciate the questions and uncertainties their methods can throw up; the second shows how **not** to use statistics!

Case Study 1: the English urban hierarchy, 1523–1801

In 1959 the landscape historian W.G. Hoskins produced a 'ranking table' of the forty-two leading English provincial towns at various dates between the fourteenth and nineteenth centuries.[3] Hoskins's lists have been widely used by urban historians and three of them are reproduced in Table 1.

Case study 1 *(continued)*

Table 1 The ranking of English provincial towns

1523–1527 (Subsidy paid: to nearest £)		1662 (Number of hearths taxed)		1801 (Census population)	
1 Norwich	1704	1 Norwich	7302	1 Manchester	84,020
2 Bristol	1072	2 York	7294	2 Liverpool	77,653
3 Newcastle	not taxed	3 Bristol	6925	3 Birmingham	73,670
4 Coventry	974	4 Newcastle	5967	4 Bristol	63,645
5 Exeter	855	5 Exeter	5294	5 Leeds	53,162
6 Ipswich	657	6 Ipswich	5020	6 Plymouth	43,194
7 Salisbury	852	7 Great Yarmouth	4750	7 Norwich	36,832
8 Lynn	576	8 Oxford	4205*	8 Bath	32,200
9 Canterbury	552	9 Cambridge	4133*	9 Portsmouth	32,166
10 Reading	c. 470	10 Canterbury	3940	10 Sheffield	31,314
11 Colchester	426	11 Worcester	3619	11 Hull	29,516
12 Bury St Edmunds	405	12 Deptford	3554	12 Nottingham	28,861
13 Lavenham	402	13 Shrewsbury	3527	13 Newcastle	28,366
14 York	379	14 Salisbury	3498	14 Exeter	17,398
15 Totnes	c. 317	15 Colchester	3414	15 Leicester	16,953
16 Worcester	312	16 East Greenwich	3390	16 Stoke-on-Trent	16,414
17 Gloucester	c. 307	17 Hull	3390	17 York	16,145
18 Lincoln	298	18 Coventry	3301	18 Coventry	16,034
19 Hereford	273	19 Chester	3004	19 Ashton-under-Lyme	15,632
20 Great Yarmouth	260	20 Plymouth	2600†	20 Chester	15,032
21 Hull	256	21 Portsmouth	2600†	21 Dover	14,845
22 Boston	c. 240	22 Lynn	2572	22 Great Yarmouth	14,845
23 Southampton	224	23 Rochester	2271	23 Stockport	14,830
24 Hadleigh	c. 224	24 Lincoln	2211	24 Shrewsbury	14,739
25 Wisbech	c. 220	25 Dover	2208	25 Wolverhampton	12,565
26 Shrewsbury	c. 220	26 Nottingham	2190	26 Bolton	12,549
27 Oxford	202	27 Gloucester	2174	27 Sunderland	12,412
28 Leicester	199	28 Bury St Edmunds	2109‡	28 Oldham	12,024
29 Cambridge	181	29 Winchester	2069‡	29 Blackburn	11,980
30 Stamford	c. 180	30 Sandwich	2033	30 Preston	11,887
31 Northampton	180	31 Maidstone	1900	31 Oxford	11,694
32 Windsor	178	32 Leeds	1798	32 Colchester	11,520
33 Plymouth	163	33 Leicester	1773	33 Worcester	11,352
34 Maldon	c. 150	34 Northampton	1610	34 Ipswich	11,277
35 St Albans	c. 150	35 Chatham	1588	35 Wigan	10,989
36 Chichester	138	36 Ely	1554	36 Derby	10,832
37 Winchester	132	37 Chichester	1550†	37 Warrington	10,567
38 Long Melford	c. 120	38 Gateshead	1532	38 Chatham	10,505
39 Sudbury	c. 120	39 Southampton	1500	39 Carlisle	10,221
40 Rochester	117	40 Derby	1479	40 Dudley	10,107
41 Nottingham	112	41 Ludlow	1467	41 King's Lynn	10,096
42 Neyland	c. 110	42 Warwick	1467	42 Cambridge	10,087

Source: W.G. Hoskins, *Local History in England*, London, 1959, pp. 238–241.

Notes: * excluding the colleges
      ‡ 1664 Lady Day assessment
      † estimate

Case study 1 *(continued)*

Look at these lists now, ignoring the figures (for the moment). **What do they tell us about the English 'urban network' at each date? Do *not* look at the subsequent discussion until you've jotted down some ideas of your own!**

I hope you've noted at least some of the following points.

The column *1523–1527* shows the developed urban network of late medieval England. Note how few of the major towns are in the north, and also the dominance of East Anglia, with sixteen out of the forty-two, reflecting the importance of its textile industry, which also explains the inclusion of West Country towns such as Totnes. Administration – both civil and ecclesiastical – is obviously an important factor in a town's success: many are county towns, the seats of bishoprics, or have wealthy abbeys. And the importance of water transport shows up clearly: most of the towns are on navigable rivers or on/near the coast.

By *1662* there have been some dramatic changes in the fortunes of individual towns. Some – e.g. Totnes, Lavenham and Long Melford – have disappeared completely. Others have gone down in the rankings (Coventry fourth to eighteenth, Lynn eighth to twenty-second, Southampton twenty-third to thirty-ninth) or up (York from fourteenth to second,[4] Yarmouth from twentieth to seventh, Cambridge from twenty-ninth to ninth). And there are some notable new arrivals, which fall into two categories:

- **dockyard towns** – Deptford, East Greenwich and Portsmouth, for example, reflecting the Cromwellian build-up of the Royal Navy
- **industrial towns** such as Leeds and Gateshead

And overall there's a slight swing towards the Midlands and the north.

The column *1801* very much shows 'England in transition'. The 'old' towns still put up quite a strong showing, but the top rankings have now gone to the industrial towns of the Midlands and north which – with the exception of Leeds – didn't figure on the previous lists. Smaller industrial centres, such as Oldham and Ashton-under-Lyme, have pushed out places like Warwick and

Case study 1 *(continued)*

Ludlow, and the 'leisure industry' (established in the 1660s, but only in its infancy) has made itself felt with the strong showing of Bath (although by this date it was less fashionable than previously, but the new seaside resorts – such as Brighton – are not yet large enough to figure). East Anglia is now dropping out of the picture, with only six of the forty-two.

So far, no statistics? Not quite true: without the figures, we couldn't have got the rankings: what we've been looking at are both **ordinal** and **interval** data. Ordinal data enable us to put things into some sort of order (e.g. we know that Cambridge had more hearths than Shrewsbury in 1662) and interval data tell us precisely **how** many (4,133 – 3,527 = 596). But our conclusions have been reached simply by using our historical skills, aided probably by our foreknowledge that the Midlands and north are going to rise at the expense of the south and east in this period.

Now go back and look at the lists again. This time, look at the figures: what immediately strikes you when you compare the three ranking tables?

If you've compared them – rather than simply running your eye down each list – you should have immediately noted that each uses a different ranking criterion. Only 1801 uses population; 1523–1527 uses 'Subsidy [i.e. tax] paid' in pounds and 1662 the number of hearths taxed. So are we comparing like with like? Might some of the ups and downs be caused not by a town's rising or declining prosperity, but simply because it might put up a better showing using one measure rather than another?

Two obvious points are that there's no guarantee that a tax levied in 1523–1527 would net the same percentage of the population as one levied on a different basis in 1662, and that a town might be 'very populous but very poor', as Daniel Defoe found in the textile centres of the Essex/Suffolk borders in the 1720s.[5] In the 1520s, presence of a handful of rich tax-payers could make a significant difference to a town's position. Coventry, rather smaller than Bristol, paid nearly as much tax in 1523–1527, thanks to three merchants who between them contributed over 25 per cent of the tax yield; Norwich's figures are inflated by Robert

Case study 1 *(continued)*

Jannys, a grocer, who paid nearly as much tax as the whole city of Rochester. As Coventry and Norwich would be expected to rank high, this might easily be missed: a more obvious anomaly is the small town of Lavenham whose high ranking was the almost unaided achievement of the Springs, also clothiers, the wealthiest provincial family outside the peerage.[6]

This can serve as a warning against taking figures at their face value. It still doesn't get us any nearer deciding whether we can, realistically, compare these lists. Ideally, we need them all to be expressed in the same unit of measurement. The obvious one to choose is **population**: can we somehow convert tax (and hearths) into people? To do this, we need a **multiplier**. Let's call this x: so looking at 1523–1527, if we multiplied Norwich's £1,704 tax yield by x we could arrive at an estimate of its population. We'd need another multiplier (y) to convert hearths into people. But what figure to choose? We need to know the following:

- the basis of assessment: was the tax paid by individuals or households?
- what was the average household size? Did this vary over time, or between regions? Might poorer towns have had smaller average household sizes? And might rapidly growing ones have a higher percentage of young unmarried (or newly married) immigrants which would also have a lowering effect?
- the proportion of tax-payers to non-tax-payers: how many people were too poor to pay? How many evaded assessment completely?

Note that these questions are **historical** rather than statistical ones. Using quantitative evidence doesn't mean you have to leave your 'historical' skills behind: rather, you're having to deploy them into new areas.

Dyer, whose main concern is investigating the alleged late medieval 'urban crisis', suggests a 1523–1527 multiplier of 6.5 as 'not unreasonable'.[7] Using this, he calculates that overall towns had lost about 12 per cent of their population since the 14th century, against a national decline of 10 per cent.

Case study 1 *(continued)*

Can you spot a weakness in this argument? We're only looking at the 'top forty-two'. We're back to the question of 'how representative'? There were over 600 towns in early Tudor England: the Hoskins figures simply show that the *larger* communities had declined, possibly because of merchants' desire to escape gild regulations, or the expensive obligations of civic office. Smaller, unregulated and unincorporated communities may have gained as a result, and the overall urban share of the population may not have decreased at all.

And what about weaknesses in the methodology? There are two I can see:

● the multiplier is critical: as Dyer himself notes 'if the . . . multiplier were to be increased quite modestly to 7.4, the loss would disappear'[8]
● whatever multiplier is used runs the risk of distorting the experience of individual towns: what works for Norwich needn't necessarily work for York, and – for the reasons noted above – would be dangerously misleading for towns such as Lavenham

So once again it's your **historical** judgement that you have to apply in order to decide whether to follow this particular line of inquiry. And the question 'how representative?' poses itself again: but may be unanswerable at national level.

At local level, however, multipliers can help to indicate population trends, as Alan Rogers showed in his work on Stamford, Lincs. There are two things to note here: Rogers was lucky in finding sources quite evenly spread throughout the period from the sixteenth to early nineteenth century, and in having some almost contemporary seventeenth- and late eighteenth-century sources to act as a check on each other. As in the exercise we've just done, Rogers was faced with reconciling various categories of information: families, communicants, houses and individuals. How he did it is shown in Table 2.

Case study 1 *(continued)*

Table 2 The population of Stamford, 1563–1801

Date	Source		Multiplier	Population
1563	Diocesan survey	213 families	4.5*	958
1603	Diocesan survey	746 communicants	1.33†	992
1674	Hearth Tax	400 houses	5.0‡	2,000
1676	Compton Census	1,594 adults	1.33§	2,120¶
c.1720	Diocesan survey	470 families	4.5*	2,115
1785	Local census	3,937 persons		3,937
c.1790	Diocesan survey	856 families	4.5*	3,852‖
1801	Census of Great Britain			4,022

Source: Alan Rogers, *Approaches to Local History*, 2nd edn (London, 1977), pp. 15–16.

Notes: * assumes average family size = 4.5 persons
  † assumes that communicants are two-thirds of the population (i.e. excludes children under 12)
  ‡ assumes that the average household consists of five persons (i.e. 'household' is larger than 'family')
  § assumes that adults represent two-thirds of the population
  ¶ Rogers gives this as 2,125
  ‖ Rogers gives this as 3,952

Look carefully at Rogers's reasoning: anything you would be dubious about? I would query the assumptions that:

● children started to take communion at 12
● adults in 1676 were two-thirds of the population
● family size remained unchanged between the sixteenth and late eighteenth century

Note that, once again, these are all **historical** rather than statistical questions. The 'communion' issue could be explored through looking at the large volume of recent work on post-Reformation religious behaviour; the proportion of adults and the size of families are covered in most work on historical demography, although if we were actually working on Stamford we would need to look at other sources – such as parish registers – to form our own conclusions.

Case study 1   *(continued)*

These points allowed, do you find his overall conclusions convincing?   I think you ought to: I do, even allowing for the two mistakes in calculation. Stamford seems to mirror what we know of national trends: there's little change in the late sixteenth to early seventeenth centuries, stagnation or slight decline in the late seventeenth to early eighteenth and quite a noticeable increase by the 1780s (the 'demographic revolution' under way). Particularly convincing is the close correlation between the 1674 and 1676 figures and those for 1785–1801

You'll notice that we've now moved to a further dimension of historical quantification. We're looking at **hypothetical statistics** (guesstimates), in other words working from figures we know so as to produce those we don't. This reflects the fact that before the nineteenth century the figures that were recorded often don't answer, directly, the questions that interest historians. So, if you were seated at the Exchequer in the sixteenth or seventeenth century, you wouldn't be greatly concerned about the population of the country, or of individual towns, but in how much money could be squeezed out of them. And if you were a seventeenth-century bishop of Lincoln, your interest in communicants would stem from fears of the spread of nonconformity, not a desire to know what was the population of Stamford.

Hypothetical statistics play a very large role in historical controversy. Inevitably, they are speculative: much depends on our methodology (i.e. using the right multiplier) which in turn depends on our understanding of the period or topic we're studying. Economic historians are the most enthusiastic devotees of this approach, largely because of the paucity of the data they're dealing with: there are lots of figures, but they're often isolated in time or place (so there's no way of checking them against any other source). There are, basically, two choices: to use them as they stand, or to try and generalise from them. 'Using them as they stand' takes us back, once again, to Clapham's 'how representative?' Just to give one example: in 1983 Peter Lindert and Geoffrey Williamson produced a highly regarded reinterpretation of living standards in the British Industrial Revolution.[9] They claim that

Case study 1 *(continued)*

the most important addition in their new 'cost-of-living' index is the addition of house rent: they add, disarmingly, that 'ours includes a few dozen cottages in Trentham, Staffordshire'.[10] By now, you should have learned to recognise the danger signs.

Case study 2: how not to do it

I'm going to stay in the period of the Industrial Revolution. In spite of decades of research, hard-and-fast figures for agricultural and industrial output are hard to come by, and so growth has to be estimated by using a variety of 'surrogate' figures based on one particular source. The problem is that this may well relate to a particular year, rather than a run of years, and there's no guarantee that the year is 'typical'. This particular branch of historical quantification has now reached high levels of sophistication, but to show the pitfalls involved, I'm taking (rather unfairly, perhaps) an early example. Phyllis Deane and W.A. Cole attempted, as part of a much wider econometric survey of the British economy since 1688, to measure the growth of corn production in eighteenth-century England.[11] They used an estimate made in 1766 by Charles Smith that the annual consumption of grain was 18 bushels per head. They recognise the problems involved here, but conclude 'it still seems plausible to assume that there was no very great change in the overall relationship between the consumption of cereals and the total population over the eighteenth century as a whole'.[12] In other words, people in 1700 were eating 18 bushels a year, and so were people in 1800. So corn output can be assessed by a series of simple calculations:

1 Multiply the population (at 10-yearly intervals) by 2.25 to give total corn consumption in quarters (the usual unit of measurement: 18 bushels = 2.25 quarters).
2 Assess the net output by adding/subtracting exports/imports.

Case study 2 *(continued)*

---

3 Add 10 per cent to net output to allow for seed corn (you have
   to be able to plant something next year).
4 Add together to achieve a final total.

Using this formula, Deane and Cole calculated that gross corn output rose from 14.8 million quarters in 1700 to 27.8 million in 1820,
with most of the increase coming after 1750: the 'agricultural
revolution' vindicated, perhaps?
   But can you spot a problem?   Apart from the assumption that
Smith's estimate holds good for the whole century, there's only
one real **variable**, introduced at stage 2, in the shape of exports
and imports. It's generally agreed that these never accounted for
more than 5 per cent of output/consumption before 1820, and so
they can't affect the overall result very much. So agricultural output **inevitably** moves in pace with population growth, and it all
becomes circular: the assumption of no change in *per capita* consumption determines the answer that the exercise is designed to
find out![13]

The next stage

This chapter has reversed the usual order of texts on quantification: it's
normal to look at principles first, and then go on to their application.
What I've tried to do is to show you that statistics are nothing to be
frightened of, provided they are treated like any other form of historical
evidence: we've seen some of their promise, and some of their
pitfalls. This may be as far as you wish to go, in which case all well and
good: but if you want to explore further, I'm afraid there's no avoiding
the language of mathematics. I guess that many of the misapprehensions
about statistics stem from failure to realise this point: once you know
the conventions, syntax and grammar, it's all relatively plain sailing. This
final section of the chapter is designed for those of you who simply want
to know a little more about quantification in order to understand the
secondary literature and – above all – for those who might want to use
quantitative methods in a dissertation or project, but are uncertain where
to start.

Let's get back to the point about 'language'. We can identify four main 'parts of speech'.[14]

Nouns symbols such as X and Y are used to represent particular quantities or variables, at least in general formulae (i.e. formulae that tell you how to carry out widely applicable statistical operations, such as standard deviation). In specific applications it's common for the initial letter of the particular variable to be used (thus P = population, for example), **always** avoiding N, which stands for the **number** of quantities or scores under consideration. So in the Hoskins ranking tables, $N = 42$.

Adjectives used when we want to identify/qualify our noun more precisely. They take the form of what's known as a **subscript**: thus X_1, X_2, etc. So the population of a county in 1851 could be P_1, in 1861 P_2 and so on. It's quite common to use words in this way: so if you were comparing county populations in a formula, P_{Cambs} and $P_{Suffolk}$ would be quite acceptable. And, for reasons to be explained shortly, X_i is very commonly used.

Verbs tell us what to do with the nouns and their attached adjectives. Most are the arithmetical symbols you know already ($+$, $-$ etc.) but one that often confuses students is $\sum$ (sigma, the Greek capital S). This simply means 'sum' (i.e. add up).

Adverbs define what to do more precisely. So, using P = population, if we wanted to show that five populations should be summed (e.g. the first five towns on the Hoskins 1801 ranking table) we could write it as $P_1 + P_2 + P_3 + P_4 + P_5$, or $P_1 + \ldots + P_5$. All very tedious: so we can use our first formula. In this case it would be:

$$\sum_{i=1}^{5} P_i$$

The notations above and below tell us we have to add together the successive values of P, starting with Manchester ($i = 1$) and ending with Leeds (5). If for some reason we wanted to exclude the top five but go down as far as Dover (21) the formula would now read:

$$\sum_{i=6}^{21} P_i$$

We can now move on to something a little more complex, in the shape of an equation. Our 'sum' instruction can be expressed in general terms as:

$$\sum_{i=1}^{N} P_i$$

Applied to our 1801 figures (this list is what's known as a 'column' vector, incidentally), this means add the whole lot up. If we wanted to find the **arithmetical mean** (i.e. the 'average') of the forty-two, we add the forty-two figures together, and then divide by 42. Our answer is the mean, usually expressed as $\bar{x}$. Can you come up with a formula to describe the operation, using the 'general' case first? You should end up with:

$$\frac{\sum_{i=1}^{N} X i}{N}$$

or

$$\bar{x} = \frac{\sum_{i=1}^{42} P_i}{N}$$

for the 1801 list.

I'm not going to take you any further in this particular direction: you should have got the general drift by now. As long as you distinguish clearly between **instructions** (e.g. $\sum$) and **variables** (e.g. X) you shouldn't have any major problems in understanding equations, or the formulae used to describe the most commonly used statistical operations.

A checklist for quantitative historians

The basic quantitative skills that you will find most useful are:

1 **knowing how to arrange your data** (e.g., frequency distributions; grouped frequency distributions; bar charts and histograms; pie diagrams)
2 **measures of central tendency** (e.g., the arithmetical mean; the median; the mode)
3 **measures of dispersion around a mean** (e.g., the semi-inter-quartile range; standard deviation)
4 **correlation** (e.g., the mean square contingency coefficient phi; Spearman's rank order correlation; the tetrachoric correlation coefficient)
5 **the analysis of time series** (e.g., rates of growth; trends; indexing and index numbers)
6 **regression analysis**
7 **sampling techniques** and the concept of 'significance'

Which of these techniques you end up using will depend partly on your own interests and partly on the type of data you are using. If you are interested in exploring further, two useful texts are: F. Clegg, *Simple Statistics*, Cambridge University Press, 1982; D. Rowtree, *Statistics Without Tears*, Penguin, 1991.

You will find, though, that many texts on statistics reflect the interests of modern statisticians, which are 'inference' and 'probability', neither of which has yet been explored to any great extent by historians. For our needs, there are two books of particular value: R. Floud, *An Introduction to Quantitative Methuen Methods for Historians* (out of print) and D.N. McCloskey, *Econometric History*, Macmillan, 1987. Floud goes carefully through all the analytical tools you are ever likely to need and explains the reasoning behind them, and what they can (and can't) do: in these days of the pocket calculator and the PC – which remove the necessity for much manual calculation – this background reasoning is especially important so that you can **understand** what you're doing and why you're doing it. And McCloskey 'humanises' econometrics by gearing this seemingly cold science to concrete historical examples in a down-to-earth, illuminating and humorous way.

But the best way to discover statistics is to join a class on the subject, as I did, more years ago than I care to recall. I must admit the major benefit I derived was a knowledge of the laws of probability which led to my family and friends refusing to play any games of chance with me. So be warned: once Scrabble becomes a mathematical battle-ground, your social life can be seriously damaged!

As more degree courses go modular, the possibilities for this sort of exploration grow. If you find that your institution offers such a course – which will typically be entitled something like 'Techniques of data handling' – go for it: you'll get expert tuition, you'll meet students from a variety of disciplines and you'll almost certainly find that your tutor will be delighted to show you how statistical techniques can be adapted to a variety of historical data. You might even end up as a cliometrician.

Notes

1   Quoted in D.N. McCloskey, *Econometric History* (London, 1987), p. 41.
2   A.W. Coats, quoted in J. Hoppit, 'Counting the Industrial Revolution', *Economic History Review*, 2 ser XLIII, 2 (1990): 189.
3   W.G. Hoskins, *Local History in England* (London, 1959), pp. 238–241.
4   Don't read too much into this. Its low ranking in 1523–1527 may have been anomalous, as it appears in the top two or three in the fourteenth-century lists.
5   Daniel Defoe, *A Tour through England and Wales*, Everyman Edition, (London, n.d.), p. 48.
6   W.G. Hoskins, 'English provincial towns in the early sixteenth century' (1963), reprinted in P. Clark (ed.) *The Early Modern Town, A Reader* (London, 1976), pp. 91–105.
7   A. Dyer, *Decline and Growth in English Towns, 1400–1640* (London, 1991), p. 39.
8   ibid.
9   Peter H. Lindert and Jeffrey G. Williamson, 'English workers' living standards during the Industrial Revolution: a new look', *Economic History Review*, 2 ser. XXXVI, 1 (1983): 1–25.
10   ibid., p. 9.
11   P. Deane and W.A. Cole, *British Economic Growth, 1688–1959*, 2nd edn, (Cambridge, 1967), pp. 63ff.
12   ibid., p. 64.
13   For a full discussion of Deane and Cole's methodology, and a useful survey of more recent attempts to measure agricultural output, see R.V Jackson, 'Growth and deceleration in English agriculture, 1660–1790', *Economic History Review*, 2 ser XXXVIII, 3 (1985): 333–351.
14   The idea of statistics as a 'language' is more fully explored by R.S. Schofield, 'Sampling in historical research', in E.A. Wrigley (ed.) *Nineteenth-century Society: Essays in the Use of Quantitative Methods for the Study of Social Data* (Cambridge, 1972), pp. 185ff. I largely follow Wrigley's definitions of the 'parts of speech' here.

Historical terms
David Weigall

One of the first things the history student discovers is how many of the words and phrases used by historians are debated or ambiguous. This is, perhaps, hardly surprising in a subject as lively and controversial as history. At the same time a proper understanding of concepts and the ability to debate ideas are key skills essential to the successful history student.

You should be aware that many of the terms below have been, and continue to be, used polemically, in argument, to persuade or oppose. What follow are brief introductory definitions of these terms.

Historical terms

Absolutism   The theory and practice of unfettered government power, particularly associated with the monarchs of the period from the sixteenth to the eighteenth century in Europe. It should be distinguished from **Totalitarianism**.

Anachronism   Importing into the past concepts and values alien to that period or culture.

Anarchism   A political philosophy which asserts that society can and should be organised without the need for coercive state power. The word 'anarchy' has been used since antiquity as a pejorative term for political, social and moral breakdown in society.

Ancien régime The 'old order' in French. The phrase used to describe the governmental and social structure of the period of absolute monarchy in Europe (see **Absolutism**) before the French Revolution of 1789.

Annales School An approach to historical study named after the *Annales d'histoire économique et sociale* founded in 1929 by Lucien Febvre (1878–1956) and Marc Bloch (1886–1944) at the University of Strasbourg, characterised by a departure from traditional narrative chronological history and the incorporation of other disciplines, particularly geography and social anthropology.

Antiquarianism Modern historical study is commonly contrasted with 'mere' antiquarianism – data collection for data collection's sake, learned curiosity devoid of interpretation. Originally 'antiquarianism' described a style of scholarship that flourished in Europe, particularly from the fifteenth to eighteenth century, devoted to the classification of relics, monuments and texts. Antiquarian methods for the classification and evaluation of evidence have made a very major contribution to historical scholarship.

Capitalism The system of economic organisation and production typical of many Western societies since the sixteenth century and especially since the **Industrial Revolution** of the eighteenth century. It is characterised by a preference for consumption and based on the calculated investment of savings for the production of new wealth. It is also used to describe any economic system, past or present, where there is a combination of private property, a relatively free and competitive market and a general assumption that the majority of the workforce will be employed by private employers engaged in producing whatever goods they can sell at a profit.

Causation The representation of historical events, conditions and processes as consequences of prior conditions and/or, human actions.

Class Before the nineteenth century social standing was defined in terms of 'rank', 'estate' and 'degree' – categories that could be defined in terms of heredity, occupation and prestige. By the early 1820s 'class' had become established as a social term. The notion of history as an arena for the conflict between social classes became a dominant theme in historical and political writings. Marx (1818–1883) and Engels (1820–1895) declared in the *Communist Manifesto* (1848) that the 'history of all hitherto existing society is the history of class struggles'. The development of sociological theory has encouraged further use of the concept of class in historical research. In recent decades the idea of class has been refined as one aspect of a larger issue of social stratification.

Cliometrics   History which makes use of mathematical and statistical theory. The cliometric approach dates from the 1950s.

Collectivism   Any political, social or economic theory or practice which encourages communal or state ownership and control of the means of production and distribution. A **Collective**, by contrast, is any group of cooperating individuals who may produce or own goods together but which does not exercise coercive power over its members.

Communism   Ideally, a type of human society characterised by common ownership of the means of production and self-government in all areas of life. Usually contrasted with **Capitalism**, Communism also describes theories justifying such a society. The communist order has usually been seen as the outcome of class conflict and revolutionary struggle, leading to the victory of the proletariat and the establishment of a classless society. (See: **Marxist interpretation of history**.)

Comparative history   An approach to historical study based on analogies between societies, institutions or different periods. In the course of the twentieth century it has developed as a branch of **Historiography** involving systematic and deliberate comparison.

Conservatism   A term which has come to cover a wide range of political movements. In general conservatives wish to preserve existing institutions and traditions, are sceptical towards proposals for radical change and idealistic notions about human nature. In recent years in particular Conservative parties have shown marked divergence between those who primarily value the principle of the defence of property and encouragement to private enterprise and individualism and, on the other hand, those who have emphasised paternalism.

Contemporary history   The history of the most recent past, the twentieth century, or more particularly events since the end of the Second World War in 1945.

Counter-factual Speculation on what would or would not have happened if a key cause or particular circumstance had not existed, or on the outcome of events which did not happen.

Crisis A short period of decisive challenge, or a crucial turning point or moment of vital decision. 'Crisis' has become a loose synonym for 'turning point'.

Cultural history Traditionally understood as the study of 'high culture', such as art and literature. In recent years there has been a significant effort to broaden cultural history to include popular culture and to recreate the group consciousness of past societies – mentalités.

Democracy A political system in which citizens directly, as in ancient Athens, or indirectly, through representatives, as in the UK in a parliamentary, or in the US, under a presidential system, decide the way they are governed. The term Democracy in its modern sense came into use in the course of the nineteenth century to describe a system of representative government in which the representatives are chosen by free competitive elections.

Demography The study and analysis of the structure and size of past populations and patterns of family life. Demographers investigate the relationship between economic and social changes and population. Historical demography has developed as a distinct branch of historical research since the 1950s.

Despotism Describes tyrannical or arbitrary government. Despotism means not only that the power is concentrated, but that the ruler is without any effective opposition within his or her own state.

Determinism The belief that history is determined by forces and conditions other than the motives and free will of individuals. This may be providence, as in the traditional Christian view, destiny or natural circumstances such as climate, geographic location or social traditions. Less commonly, Determinism describes the view that events are the unavoidable results of definite causes. An influential example of determinism is the **Marxist interpretation of history**.

Dialectic In its modern sense the term was defined by the Prussian philosopher Hegel (1770–1831) and adapted by Karl Marx (1818–1883).

It has come to mean a style of thought or broad approach to historical explanation which represents social change in terms of tensions, contradictions and conflicts.

Dialectical materialism The most fundamental doctrine of Marxist philosophy concerned with the general laws of change and development in thought, nature and society. Dialectical materialism attaches crucial importance to the successive and progressive struggle of opposites, 'thesis' and 'antithesis', being resolved in 'synthesis'. It postulates that matter is primary and that the material world alone is real, while ideas and thought are secondary or simply reflections or derivative of material reality.

Fascism Term employed to explain various non-socialist forms of nationalistic authoritarianism in the twentieth century. More specifically, it refers to the political doctrine advanced by the Italian Duce Benito Mussolini (1883–1945) which spread to other parts of Europe in the inter-war years. Fascism was militantly nationalistic, authoritarian, anti-liberal, anti-socialist and anti-democratic. In the post-war era the word 'neo-fascist' has been used to describe what are regarded as successors to the fascist movements in Italy, Germany and elsewhere.

Feminist historiography The study of history with particular emphasis on the experience of women. Feminist historiography has been particularly informative in its researches into the role of domestic labour and the construction of gender roles. An earlier emphasis on the recovery of women's contribution to and place in history has led on to an analysis which challenges male perceptions of history and society and patriarchal assumptions.

Feudalism Describes the network of social obligations among the aristocracy of medieval Europe and the relations of the nobility with the agricultural producers under their control. Feudalism was characterised by production for use rather than exchange and by the relative absence of wage labour or freedom of movement for those working on the land.

Gender The social aspect of the relations between the sexes.

Historical materialism The belief that material or physical conditions fundamentally influence historical events and developments. See also **Marxist interpretation of history**.

Historicity   Historical particularity, the condition of being place- and time-specific.

Historicism   Most frequently understood in English as a description of the view that the study of history can lead to the discovery of general laws of social development and may be used to predict future events.

Historiography   Used in two senses. The broader definition covers written history in general and the act of writing history. More narrowly, it is used to describe the study of the history of historical writing and interpretation.

Ideology   A term which appeared first during the French Revolution (1789–1799). Originally defined as 'the science of ideas', it soon came to mean the system of ideas, outlook and attitudes of a particular society or social group. On the popular level it has become a synonym for 'political creed'. Marxist historians have commonly used the word to describe political and social beliefs that reflect narrow class interests and constitute a one-sided view of reality.

Imperialism   The desire, from a range of motives – strategic, economics, prestige, missionary, pressure of population – to build up an empire. The word was first used to describe the ambitions of Napoleon I (1769–1821). In current usage 'imperialism' is very frequently used in a pejorative way, suggesting an illegitimate extension of power and influence over other peoples.

Industrialisation   The change in methods of production responsible for the greatly increased wealth-creating capacity of modern societies. The major characteristics of industrialisation are division of labour, the factory system and the application of scientific method to productivity.

Industrial Revolution   Used particularly to refer to the changes in the British economy between *c.* 1750 and *c.* 1850, the first economy to experience these changes in the modern period. The term is also used to describe other periods of rapid technological and organisational change in methods of production.

Interdisciplinary history   Historical scholarship and writing which makes use of concepts and methods of subjects other than history. (The

Annales School is a good example of this openness to the methods and findings of other disciplines.)

Liberalism This refers either to the belief of a particular party or a general social and political attitude emphasising the preservation of individual rights, freedom of choice, toleration and a belief in limited, constitutional, government.

Marxist interpretation of history Also known as '**Historical materialism**' – the interpretation of history as the result, above all, of the economic development of society, of the division of society into mutually hostile classes. According to Marx (1818–1883) modern society was divided into the bourgeoisie which controlled capital and the proletariat which sold its labour for wages. History was seen as the history of class conflict.

Modernisation Describes the process through which a traditional and pre-technological society passes as it is transformed into a society characterised by machine technology and a highly differentiated social structure.

Narrative Telling history in story form.

Nationalism The political belief that a group of people representing a national community sharing a language, culture, race and common history should live under one political system and be independent of others. It also often involves the claim that, so constituted – as a nation-state – they can be regarded as of equal standing with others in the world order.

Objectivity This means two things in historical scholarship: (1) impartiality; and (2) adherence to critical standards and methods. It does not require absence of value judgement; and realistically cannot.

Oral history History based on oral evidence. Note, though, that the distinction between oral and documentary evidence is not absolutely clear-cut. Much written evidence is the result of earlier oral traditions.

Periodisation The division of the past into separate periods. Historians find this unavoidable for reasons of convenience but Periodisation is often arbitrary.

Philosophy of history   This can mean two very different things. First it describes the attempt to establish a pattern or meaning in history, frequently as the expression of some universal design. Second, it signifies the study of history as a body of knowledge, through the critical analysis of historical writings and methods.

Positivism   The belief that the method of natural science provides the principal, or even the sole, model for the attainment of true knowledge. Supporters of positivism have claimed, for instance, that history is not the place for **Value judgements**.

Progress   The belief in a pattern of continuous improvement in society, of the cumulative advance of civilisation.

Prosopography   A historical method involving the systematic study of individual lives and careers, family relationships and patronage. It is particularly associated with the pioneering work of Sir Lewis Namier (1888–1960) in his detailed structural analysis of eighteenth-century British parliaments.

Radical history   History written in conscious support of progressive political and social change, and in opposition to perceived injustice and inequality.

Recurrence   The belief that history repeats itself and that lessons can be learned from the study of past events.

Relativism   The view that knowledge and understanding of the past are inevitably limited by the perspective, values and prejudices of the author.

Renaissance   Meaning 'rebirth', this term was first used to describe the revival of art and literature, and interest in classical antiquity, in Italy between the fourteenth and sixteenth centuries. Historians have discerned earlier 'renaissances', such as those of the eighth and twelfth centuries.

Revisionism   A term applied originally by Marxists to attempt to reassess the basic tenets of revolutionary socialism. It has come to mean the questioning of earlier interpretations and certainties. It is also commonly used to refer to the revision of territorial boundaries.

Revolution   A radical and fundamental change in thought, system of government, or mode of production, e.g. scientific revolution, French Revolution, or **Industrial Revolution**. The word has been, and is, used so extensively that it has been devalued.

Secularisation   The process, especially evident in modern industrial societies, through which religious practices, institutions and beliefs lose social significance.

Social Darwinism   From the late nineteenth century, especially in Britain and the US, Social Darwinism translated the idea of the survival of the fittest into a social theory. Social Darwinists argued that social organisations are like living organisms. Only by continuous development can societies maintain their cohesion and defend themselves.

Socialism   A political doctrine that emerged during the **Industrialisation** of Europe. Socialism traditionally aspires to a classless society with the means of production owned and controlled by the community and the production effort directed to public good rather than private gain.

Sovereignty   Refers both to supreme authority over a territory and independence from any external authority.

Totalitarianism   A concept used since the 1930s to describe in particular the regimes of Nazi Germany, Fascist Italy and the Soviet Union. Utilising advanced methods of mass communication, education, control and modern technology, a totalitarian system is an attempt to control every aspect of the life of a society, private as well as public. It involves domination by one party and **Ideology** under dictatorial leadership. The aim of 'total' control distinguished the most extreme forms of twentieth-century authoritarianism from older forms of **Despotism**, since earlier forms were not concerned with, or capable of, actively mobilising the entire population.

Universal history   The attempt to describe the history of the human race as a whole. A famous example is the *Essai sur l'histoire universelle* (1754) by Voltaire (1694–1778). There have been a number of popular contemporary historical syntheses, but this genre of historical writing has become less inviting as a consequence of increasing academic specialisation and the abundance of new knowledge about the past.

Urban history   Is particularly concerned with **Demography** and the process of urban organisation.

Value judgement   The assessment of either the past or present actions, customs or institutions from the perspective of some either stated or unstated moral viewpoint or norm.

Weltanschauung (German)   The world view or outlook of a particular society or group.

Whig interpretation of history   A term popularised by the Cambridge historian Herbert Butterfield (1900–1979) in a book with this title in 1931. Butterfield criticised as 'Whig historians' those who wrote history with an eye to the present and who were excessively preoccupied with the evolution of political, religious and civil liberties and progress. Historians, he argued, should study the past for its own sake instead of using it to justify the present.

Zeitgeist (German)   Spirit of the age.

Bibliography

The following books are recommended for further detail and more extended clarification of concepts and terms:

Bogdanor, V. (ed.) (1991) *The Blackwell Encyclopedia of Political Science*, Oxford, Basil Blackwell.

Cannon, J. (ed.) (1988) *The Blackwell Dictionary of Historians*, Oxford, Basil Blackwell.

Krieger, J. (ed.) (1993) *The Oxford Companion to the Politics of the World*, Oxford, Basil Blackwell.

Kuper, A. and J. (eds) (1985) *The Social Science Encyclopedia*, London, Routledge.

McClean I. (1996) *Oxford Concise Dictionary of Politics*, Oxford, Oxford University Press.

Outhwaite, W. and Bottomore, T. (eds) (1993) *The Blackwell Dictionary of Twentieth Century Social Thought*, Oxford, Blackwell.

Ritter, H. (1986) *Dictionary of Concepts in History*, New York, Greenwood Press.

Scruton, R. (1982) *A Dictionary of Political Thought*, London, Macmillan.